ON GOLF

.

ALSO BY TIMOTHY O'GRADY

Curious Journey:
An Oral History of Ireland's Unfinished Revolution
(with Kenneth Griffith)

Motherland

I Could Read the Sky
(with photographs by Steve Pyke)

Light

ON GOLF

.

The Game, the Players, and a

Personal History of Obsession

Timothy O'Grady

THOMAS DUNNE BOOKS

St. Martin's Press

New York

THOMAS DUNNE BOOKS.
An imprint of St. Martin's Press.

www.stmartins.com

Photos courtesy of Timothy O'Grady
Design by Kathryn Parise

ISBN 0-312-33004-9
EAN 978-0-312-33004-0

First Edition: June 2005

10   9   8   7   6   5   4   3   2   1

For Edward J. O'Grady

CONTENTS

.

ACKNOWLEDGMENTS

.

I would like to thank Steve Carr for his help on many occasions in acquiring information and for reading the manuscript. Geoff Mulligan, at the time working at *Esquire* in London, was the first to ask me to write about golf. Robert Green, Rosie Boycott, Melanie Garrett, as well as Steve Carr, sent me to play on great courses and to interview great players. The late Harry Campbell supplied me with an important book and was the Scot I had in mind when writing page 4. Nick Groom sent me Thomas Mathison's poem mentioned on page 84. Doc Giffen arranged the round with Arnold Palmer and the conversation with him that appears in the last chapter. The joke about the petulant American and his Scots caddy on page 31 appeared in James Dodson's book *Final Rounds*. My accountant, mentioned on page 80 in connection with his story about the club secretary, is Frank Dunphy. My golfing friend I refer to here and there and whose spectacular dream of murder with a sand wedge I recount on pages 164–165 is Gary McKeone. The journalist who conducted the interview with Earl Woods mentioned on page 95 is Lawrence Donegan. Bob Atkins provided the sequence of photographs of me hitting a five iron on a par three in Palm Springs that appear in this book. I had long wished to write a book about golf without knowing what it might be, until Dan Franklin at Random House in London told me about a series of books about sports written by novelists. Rachel Cugnoni invited me to write this one, Tristan Jones edited it with acute sensitivity, and Peter J. Wolverton had the idea of and suggestions for this ampler American edition.

We saw elderly citizens playing at the old Scots game of golf, which is a kind of gigantic variety of billiards.

—Peter Morris,

from *Peter's Letters to His Kinsfolk* (1819)

In this game you got eighteen holes
To shoot your best somehow.
Where have all my divots gone?
I'm on the back nine now.

Golf clubs are made of wood and iron,
They are not magic wands.
Balls drop in the sand trap.
Balls drop into ponds.
Oh, balls drop into ponds. . . .

I don't know about you, but I got to have me a few
When I get to that clubhouse bar.
It's my reward for this scorecard.
I'm way over par.
Oh mercy, I'm way over par. . . .

—Loudon Wainwright III

They become addicted immediately. We call golf "green opium."

—Ye Hong, owner of the

Beautiful Pine Driving Range, near Beijing

ON GOLF

.

1

.

The Shot

It is nearly impossible to hit a pure golf shot. Let us say that you are of similar dimensions and constitution to me. The ball, the smallest in sport save Ping-Pong balls and marbles, lies on some problematic surface of grass, weed, sand, or asphalt around six feet away from your eyes at the end of a long, slender stick that you are clutching probably with a haunted uncertainty and a turbulent viscera. This little ball weighs 1.62 ounces and is 5.28 inches in circumference. Let us say that the stick that you have in your hands is my nearly antique Wilson-manufactured Walter Hagen blade four iron, its face from hosel to toe measuring 2.7 inches along its base. For you to execute the shot, the head of this four iron must be drawn away from the ball and travel through an arc of some 270 degrees up and around your body and then return along a nearly identical path to make the strike, a distance of 47.12 feet. The action is not merely back and forward, like a pendulum or billiard stroke, but is also multiply rotating, with shoulders, hands, and hips all turning to different degrees. And all turn on a moving axis, even the shoulders, for the shift in weight to the back and then forward for the strike causes the central axis of the body to shift. Both shoulders and hands rotate ninety degrees to the right and then around one hundred and ten degrees to the left by the time of impact, with the clubface in consequence opening and closing to the same degree as the hands turn, but the timing of the rotation of the shoulders is entirely different from that of the hands, which lag considerably behind the shoulders, completing almost the entirety of the return rotation, to the point of impact, in the final 5 percent or so of the duration of their and the clubhead's journey to the ball.

You will have begun this curiously ungainly action from a position of dead stillness, but by the time you strike the ball the clubhead will be traveling at just under a hundred miles per hour. To deliver a solid blow to the ball, the correct 0.049 square inches of the clubface must meet a theoretical point on the surface of the ball, a point that might realistically be described as comprising around a tenth of the area of the nail on your little finger. The ball will stay on the clubface for only .00045 seconds before beginning its unpredictable journey. If the correct part of the clubface meets the correct part of the ball, you will make a solid impact, but this will not necessarily result in a successful shot, for the line of the clubface must be precisely perpendicular to the proposed line of flight to the flag, which rests around 180 yards away from where you are standing. An error of two degrees in alignment will result in the ball missing its target by around twenty feet to the left or right. Missing the center of the clubface by a quarter of an inch will reduce the distance the ball travels by 7 to 9 percent, or up to 48.6 feet. Each ounce of body weight wrongly transferred, each millisecond of mistiming, each mismade movement and lapse of concentration, will deposit your ball deeper into trouble, raise your score, and compound your feelings of anguish and humiliation and abject worthlessness. Practice can help make your swing more consistent, but you will never reach infallibility, or anything approaching it, for a golf swing is not repeatable. It has been demonstrated empirically that, in terms of neuromuscular activity, the action of raising a glass from table to mouth will not be repeated once in a thousand attempts, nor, of course, will even a single one of the great multitude of actions involved in a golf swing.

The golf swing is an imponderable. In the gravity and stillness of the address position, and in the spindliness of the long, thin, ineffectual-looking club at the end of extended arms, there is something of the poised heron in water. The upturned chin and protruding posterior give it a taint of the obscene. When finally the mechanism lurches into motion, anything can happen—assemblages of flails, flinches, slides, quivers, jerks, and spasms. Some swings have so many independently moving parts that they look like early pieces of farm machinery. All of them are signatures inscribed in the air—revealers of the golfing personality. Very often what they reveal is fear.

You are somewhere out on a golf course as you face this shot. You will have begun your journey of eighteen holes some five miles and four hours from where you will eventually complete it. Let us say that you are on a long par four measuring 440 yards and that you gave it a good drive of 260 yards to the center of the fairway, leaving you with this 180-yard four iron. If the fairway is forty yards wide, and the rough that can reasonably be said to belong to this hole is ten yards deep to either side, and if we add on another ten yards behind the green, then the total area of the hole would be around twenty-seven thousand square yards. The little hole that is your destination has a diameter of 4.25 inches. To make the par that you now tremulously demand of yourself, you must cause the ball to traverse this vast area and find its way into the little hole in four blows. As Arnold Haultain says in his fine little book *The Mystery of Golf,* "A tennis player has a whole court in which to play; a cricketer a whole field; the golfer has to put his ball into a hole of the size of a jam-pot, a quarter of a mile away."

Depending upon where you are playing as you stand over this shot, you might be facing, as I have at various times of my golfing life, sand, a pond or river, trees of tropical, Mediterranean, or Nordic origin, heat, rain, snow, wind, a cliff face, ocean or mountainside, scrubland such as is normally only seen in cowboy films, a glacier, ankle-clutching vegetation, cacti, a lava bed, wild elk, alligators, ball-stealing monkeys, bears, or the screamed blasphemies of bare-torsoed, potbellied, knobbly-kneed, beer-can-strewing citizens who should be required to submit themselves to the tutelage of an experienced Scots links player before they are again allowed onto a golf course. If your play on this day is variable and the match is intense, you might pass through a range of emotion in the course of the round such as could otherwise take you a month to experience. You might even pass through such a range of emotion on this single shot.

To help you make your way around the golf course taking the least number of strokes, you are allowed fourteen different clubs, each designed to advance the ball a specific distance or, in the case of the sand wedge and putter, out of or over a specific surface. You must know the distance you hit each of these clubs depending on the surface you are hitting off and the combination of climatic, emotional, and physical conditions prevailing in or around your being at the time. These variables are compounded greatly in the case of the professional, who can hit each club in fine gradations of distance and high or low or with draw or fade according to what the shot requires. The variety of shots demanded of a golfer is more multitudinous than in any other ball-striking game. In fact no golfer will ever face precisely the same shot twice.

As you play your round, you will look upon these clubs, as you will look upon your own body, as your enemies or your friends according to the state of your mind, for mind is all in golf. To hit this particular 180-yard four iron or any other golf shot, all the technicalities of the swing must be internalized in the muscles, the thinking process must be shut down, and the mind must apprehend the ball with an intense purity and concentration. When a professional instructs a beginner to keep his eye on the ball, he is doing so not for mechanical reasons or for the purpose of orientation, but rather to direct the student toward a simple, uncluttered, yet hyperaware state of mind. If obscure thoughts about the pronation of your wrists, where your hands are at the top of your backswing, or the rotation of your hips begin to rise into your mind like birds flushed from grass, or if you veer into the caves of doubt or fear or the sense of futility or even ridiculousness, then you must have at your disposal some mechanism that stops thought again and allows the mind simply to see. This is not easy. Temples and rented rooms all over the world are full of students of meditation striving for a similar effect. You can learn a great deal about how ugly and cacophonous can be the music of your mind by waiting for a moment of panic and disorientation on a golf course and then observing what is happening in your head. You are unlikely to have to wait long. It is like the sound of a shortwave radio as you move through the bands.

At the beginning of his very entertaining book *The Bogey Man*, George Plimpton constructs an elaborate and astonishing metaphor for this condition. He imagines his own body as he stands over a golf ball as a fourteen-story-high structure full of chambers and passageways and measuring instruments populated by a throng of Japanese navy men—lazy and dissolute enlisted men in the limbs and joints and lower reaches, and excitable, rice-wine-drinking admirals gathered on the galleries behind the eyes. "In their hands," he writes, "they hold ancient and useless voice tubes into which they yell the familiar orders: 'Eye on the ball! Left arm stiff! Flex the knees!' "—these instructions drifting through the huge structure until they arrive in garbled form at the drunk and distracted men, who in response reach up from their stupors and pull a few levers, sending the whole apparatus lurching and tipping until it finally strikes the ball, the admirals then clutching each other as they look out of their gallery windows and shout, "A shank! A shank! My God, we've hit another shank!"

Weather, hazards, lack of technique or practice, poor coordination, erratic biorhythms, hangovers, an unruly mind, and statistical improbability—these are just a few of the obstacles to hitting a pure golf shot. It is no wonder that Ben Hogan, considered by many to be the finest striker of the ball in the history of golf, once said, "This is a game of misses. The guy who misses the best is going to win." In the whole of Tiger Woods's miraculous millennial season, during which he won three consecutive major championships, he believed he hit only one shot of which he could be particularly proud. It took place on the fourteenth hole at St. Andrews during the British Open, which he won by eight shots. He had around 260 yards to the pin, a tight lie in the rough, and a left-to-right breeze. Pot bunkers guarded the green. He had to hit a high draw against the direction of the breeze that would carry nearly the entire distance and then land softly. The shot was blind and he had to line it up against a television crane. He selected a three wood and hit the ball with a perfect purity, the ball following the line of the crane, drawing in and then dropping down onto the green close to the pin. There are of course few people on this earth capable of realistically contemplating such a shot, let alone being able to hit it. For most golfers, hitting a four iron 180 yards to within ten feet of the hole would be one of the most significant and memorable events of the week in which it happened.

The shot is the irreducible unit of golf, and though touring professionals must think of the 270 or so of them they will strike in the course of a tournament, for most golfers the single shot is what they define and redefine themselves by. A shot stands alone in the memory. It is part of the longer story of the hole and round, but it is also an end unto itself. It can be a calamitous outrage or a magnificence that seems to resonate through the years like a poem of great beauty. Let us move back to the moments preceding the hypothetical 180-yard four iron that began this discussion. The day is fine— bright, warm, just the smallest of sea breezes to cool and caress you. Your play as usual has been inconsistent, but you have just had the pleasure of that fine 260-yard drive with a slight draw into the heart of the fairway. The hole, as do all holes, had asked of you a question on the tee, and you had answered at least this part of it well. You allow yourself the thought that perhaps this drive marked the beginning of something, that your game is about to find its focus, you are now finally going to play to your potential. Then you silence this thought. One shot at a time, you think. Don't get ahead of yourself. You walk forward with your playing companions. The ball glistens in the sunlight. You pace off the distance from the 150-yard marker. You check the direction of the breeze, the position of the flag. You remember the roll of the green. You take in all these variables, select your target, then draw your four iron out of the bag and stand over the ball. Feet, hips, shoulders, square to the line of flight. Weight evenly distributed. Right elbow close to the body. Smooth tempo. Years of reading, thinking, and practicing form the history of this shot. Though you have hit thousands of golf shots in your life, what your playing companions will see if they look at your face is a look of intensity and hope, as if this experience is unique, and much depends on it. You take the club back and then move into the ball. In this moment you experience a vertigo-inducing transformation, an instant and viciously relentless physical breakdown, as though your body has been miswired. All its parts seem engaged in distinct, unrelated activities. Your breathing is wrong. You are temporarily blind. You hear the club thud into the earth half a foot behind the ball. Your wrists vibrate painfully and all motion stops. A divot the size of a toupee flies up. As your sight is restored, you see the ball galumphing like a drunk along the fairway before coming to rest forty yards from where you are standing.

You may be able to accept this. You may think that if you hit the next shot well enough, you can still manage a par. You may even laugh. But then again you may not. A violent and enraged self-loathing may enter you like a poison injected into a vein. The excruciating ugliness of the shot has insulted the father who taught you, the years you have played the game, the true abilities you believe you possess, and most particularly your splendid drive. You may feel like tearing your liver out.

This feeling will almost certainly pass, or at least subside, quickly. After a hole or two, after a few middling strikes, you will still remember the shot, but most of the sting will have gone out of it. It will reside in you like a recently completed illness, still faintly debilitating but no longer of much relevance as you look forward again with appetite and hope toward your next shot. But then there are those rounds in which this is your fate shot after shot. Skulls, shanks, snap hooks, pop ups, jerked putts—all the vocabulary of misery around the entire eighteen holes. Memory does not dispose of such occasions so efficiently. They can stay with you like a virus. You can be walking along the street feeling reasonably all right and the thought of an entirely hideous round of golf three weeks earlier will steal up on you and lay you low.

Then there are the glorious shots. A long drive will give you a feeling of power and majesty. If it is a long drive from an elevated tee against a dramatic, mountainous background, you also get the exhilarating sensation of flight, as if the ball were a piece of yourself. There is the delicacy of touch you can demonstrate to yourself by holing a downhill, breaking ten-foot putt that you need in a match. Bending a low, punched four iron under and around the branches of trees and up to the green can temporarily convince you that you are an artist. But the most glorious of them all for me are long to middle irons that fly directly at a well-protected flag. The memory of these can stay alive for years. Every golfer has them. Golf is unusual among sports in this. A mediocre athlete cannot hit a tennis ball 140 miles per hour, go airborne from the free-throw line and slam-dunk a basketball, or run one hundred meters in less than ten seconds, no matter how many times he may attempt it. But from 150 yards or less, virtually any golfer is capable at some point of hitting a shot that feels sublime and looks as good as anything he sees professionals doing on television. Golf, of course, is not the only thing in life that offers rich, profound and important experiences, but the feeling derived from a fine golf shot is unique. For most of us, certainly, it is rare. But rarity alone is not what gives the feeling its definition.

A fine golf shot is succinct. It is simple. It is unambiguous, indisputable, and pure. The mind seems to clear a space in the memory around such a shot, so that you remember the moments before
as well as the shot itself—the assessment of what it requires, the se-
lection of the club, the silence as you stand over the ball. You draw
the club back, and as you begin the downswing, everything seems
to be moving a little slower than usual, the ball seems large and to be
seen with a particular clarity, you are more aware of your body and
the unexpectedly wonderful synchronization of feet, hips, shoulders, hands. The club is one with the rest of you and weighs virtually nothing at all. You feel entirely balanced and in possession of
what you are doing. You feel clean, lucid, strong. You have a simple
yet uncanny hyperawareness of where everything around you is, as
though your vision has extended to 360 degrees. Your hands move
down, the shaft kicks forward and drives the clubhead down and
into the back of the ball, the smell of earth rises up as the divot flies,
and from out of the corner of your eye you can see the ball leave the
club, its launch powerful, true, explosive. You feel the unimprov-
able solidity of the shot in your hands, your chest, and down near
the base of your spine before it rises up your nerves into your brain.
Your head lifts. Your hands are high, your muscles loose, your bal-
ance intact, as you watch the ball flying wonderfully, beautifully,
straight at the flag. You know that the shot is all that it can be from
you, if only the club is right. You may feel many things in this
moment—delight, physical fulfillment, modesty or its opposite, for
example. One of them, whether you care to display or even admit
it, is also likely to be astonishment.

A golf shot happens in the moment, and in the moment it can overwhelm all the anxieties and miseries in your life and seem to define the essence of the best part of what you are. Once you have made it, it is your possession. At least some small part of you can thereafter be described by it. In *Rabbit Run,* John Updike writes of Harry Angstrom hitting the drive of his life and creating a wordless metaphor in the sky in answer to the Reverend Eccles's question about what is missing in his marriage: "He looks at the ball, which sits high on the tee and already seems free of the ground. Very simply he brings the clubhead around his shoulder into it. The sound has a hollowness, a singleness he hasn't heard before. His arms force his head up and his ball is hung way out, lunarly pale against the beautiful black-blue of storm clouds, his grandfather's color stretched dense across the north. It recedes along a line straight as a ruler-edge. Stricken; sphere, star, speck. It hesitates, and Rabbit thinks it will die, but he's fooled, for the ball makes its hesitation the ground of a final leap: with a kind of visible sob takes a last bite of space before vanishing in falling. 'That's it!' he cries and, turning to Eccles with a grin of aggrandizement, repeats, 'That's it!' "

A single fine shot is the seduction that will lure you back to the course, and repeated seductions will rapidly escalate into the monomania of obsession. Golf was, I think, my first obsession. It struck me around the age of twelve. In this sense I suppose it taught me what obsession is and resonated within all the other obsessions that have governed, enriched, and distorted my life since then. There is a recklessness in obsession, and also at times an amorality, but above all there is a deep immersion in infinitesimal detail. Throughout my teenage years I practiced and played golf, I earned my wages from it, I read and talked and dreamed about it and pondered it in a way and to a degree that I did no other thing—until I fell in love when I was eighteen with a girl named Ruth Farrell and the lure of golf receded from its eminence. To love was later added writing and still later children, and golf was thereafter in a more congested space within my being. Yet at no time has it been any less than fascinating to me. I can and always could converse about it for hours, even days, without a diminishing of the fascination.

To those not similarly stricken, such talk is of course absurd and excruciating. Words such as *sublime, majestic, genius,* and *heroic* applied to men wearing clothes more suited to schoolboys as they bat a little ball around overgroomed land seem to them pathetic and contemptible. "You'd think it was something important," they say. "You'd think there were lives at stake." And when you look at them blankly and return to your feverish description of the incredible shot Tiger Woods hit at the fifteenth hole at Augusta, they run from the room with their fingers in their ears. I know one elegantly framed woman who approached the game but then could not bring herself to hit a shot. "All that 'bend over, grip the club, stick your bottom out,'" she said. "I couldn't go on. It just seemed too ridiculous." But as Arnold Haultain points out, "Golf is like faith: it is the substance of things hoped for, the evidence of things not seen; and not until it is personally experienced does the unbelieving change from the imprecatory to the precatory attitude."

Golf simply catches you and you are thereafter in some way betrothed. I know of nothing else outside of life's elementals of work, love, sex, family, that is like it. It will find your addiction gene even more rapidly than vodka or roulette wheels. I sometimes think that those taking their first timorous swings on the practice ground should be warned that once the initial barrier is passed, there is no way back. There is just something so simply wonderful about being in good company in the open air with the sun on your back, the birds singing, and the aromas of nature floating around you as you hit golf shots that fly high over the land straight at their targets. For a hole or two as the ball rises out of the heart of the club shot after shot, the game seems beautifully simple. It also seems, in some remote yet tantalizing way, conquerable. You think to yourself, Maybe I can get there. The game becomes a quest. Everything about it becomes fascinating. It is the illusion of mastery that drives the obsession.

My father also had this obsession, and it was from him that I inherited it. One day, he told me, he played seventy-two holes on a nine-hole course and was so exhausted afterward that he couldn't raise himself out of the bath. What would any normally constituted bystander have thought as he watched my father come around again to the first tee for the fifth, sixth, seventh, and eighth times, reaching into his pocket to pay his green fee on each occasion? Perhaps he enjoyed his obsession more richly than have I, for at his best he was a better player than I am (so far), and I think he had a better character for it. We spoke about golf together from the time it first gripped me until the time of his death. Our last conversations were about golf. Golfers speak about fine courses, technique, the achievements of the great and the lesser achievements of themselves. But the most entertaining talk about golf is anecdotal. My father had many stories about golf, and I believe he was skilled at the telling of them.

One of them was about a man named C. J. Bansbach, who had several times been club champion at the Butterfield Country Club in Chicago in the 1940s and '50s. I don't believe I ever met C. J. Bansbach, but I heard about him often and knew he had a thin mustache, wore plus fours, and was a fine player. Prior to my birth my father had also been a member at the Butterfield Country Club and had competed against C. J. Bansbach many times. The story concerned the death of C. J.'s father. The wake was held at a Chicago funeral home, which my father attended. He approached the coffin where the body was laid out, said a prayer, and then turned to C. J. to offer his condolences. C. J. thanked him gravely and asked my father if he would mind coming with him for a moment as he wished to have a private word. My father followed him through the mourners to a separate room. He didn't know what to expect, but he was prepared to help his friend in whatever way he could. C. J. closed the door, stood in the center of the room, and then bent over, holding in his hands an imaginary golf club. He then looked up at my father with the helpless expression of the addict and began, "Do you think if I were to move my right hand a little bit under the shaft . . . ?"

2

·

Father and Son

My father was a fine player, but his game suffered from the troubling of my birth.

He was, at the time, forty-five years old. At his best he had played off a three handicap and when I was born would have been no worse, I imagine, than a five, or perhaps six. Butterfield, where he was then a member, was out on the west side of Chicago not far from where he was born and raised, but when he married, he moved with my mother to an apartment on the north side, more than an hour's drive away from the course. Golf at the level at which he was playing requires considerable maintenance. He was driving out to Butterfield Saturdays and Sundays and sometimes on Wednesday afternoons while my mother stayed home with me.

He thought this unfair to her, so he resigned from his membership. "I did it in the winter," he told me later. "It was less painful."

For some time he was a golfing vagrant, playing occasionally at public courses or at clubs when he was invited. At weekends he went to supermarkets, amusement parks, or for walks in the forest with my mother and me, betraying no sign of a longing to be elsewhere. Sometimes he hit balls during the long summer evenings at a driving range. Finally he joined a club attached to a course in the grounds of a U.S. navy airbase not far from where we lived. The course was acceptable, but no more, and the golf played there somehow less serious, less fun, and less important for him than it had been at Butterfield. His handicap drifted slowly upward to nine. Something irreplaceable had gone from his precision of striking, his competitive edge, and his touch, and this had happened because of me.

He was the middle of three children of a man and woman who had emigrated from small farms in county Kerry in the southwest of Ireland and then met and married in Chicago. My grandfather worked twelve hours per day, seven days per week, as a streetcar conductor. He would, I imagine, have known little of golf beyond that it existed and was played by others in places somewhere outside his orbit. He had been born and raised on Lamb's Head in Caherdaniel, then a scattering of small white, thatched houses set into rocky hills around a deep, gullet-shaped beach of pale, delicate sand, mountains just behind pressing in on the sea. It is for me the most thrillingly beautiful place in Ireland. Eight miles along the road, on a sandy headland at Waterville, is one of Ireland's finest links, built just after my grandfather emigrated but tended now by one of his grandnephews, Vincent Clifford, part-time farmer and part-time greenskeeper. There are times as you walk down the fairways of Waterville that you can feel as if you were on an avenue in Manhattan, the dunes towering above you to either side. Had the course existed before my grandfather left for America, it is highly unlikely he would have played it, for golf in British colonial outposts in the late nineteenth century was generally not played by native fishermen and subsistence farmers.

My father's introduction to golf came when he began to caddy at Westward Ho!, a peculiar name that sounds like the title of a wagon train movie but in fact paid homage to England's first golf course. Caddies have traditionally been allowed to play at American clubs on Mondays, when the courses are closed to members, so I suppose that is how he first took up the game. I don't know the rate at which he advanced, but I know from a story told me by a friend of his that he was deep in the obsession in his midtwenties.

This friend's family had a house on a lake in Wisconsin around one hundred miles from Chicago, and the two of them went there once for a weekend. They were to play a match on the Sunday, but the night before they went from drinking hole to drinking hole and then to an all-night dance before winding up at a roadside diner for breakfast. At one point during their meal my father left to visit the outside toilet. He was gone for a long time. Finally his friend went out onto the porch to look for him. He heard some low moaning, looked down, and discovered my father entangled in the shrubs to the side of the stairs. Evidently the prohibition moonshine they had been drinking had unbalanced him. He was in considerable pain. They discovered later that he had cracked a rib. His friend got him back to the house and into bed and then went to sleep himself. He was awakened some hours later by a swishing sound in the living room. When he went out, he found my father swinging a golf club with one arm. "What are you doing?" he said. "We have a match," said my father. "But you can't play," said his friend. "You're injured." "I think I can manage if I just use one arm," said my father, and resumed practicing. According to his friend, they did go to a golf course and play a match, which he says my father won. I find this last detail not very credible, but I can appreciate the motivation for including it, for he told me the story just a month after my father died and he knew how susceptible I was to accounts of his rakishness and heroism.

I think it was an opportunity presented by an injury incurred during the Second World War that drove his handicap down to the serious number of three. He was a thirty-six-year-old dentist in love with but not yet married to my mother at the time of the Japanese attack on Pearl Harbor, but he immediately enlisted in the U.S. navy. He went through basic training and was then seconded to the marines for their operations in the Pacific. During a landing at Guadalcanal he injured his back climbing down the side of a ship. He was put in a makeshift medical unit in a cave on the island and then sent to New Zealand for a laminectomy, an operation to remove portions of damaged disk that have slid out from between the vertebrae and come to press on the sciatic nerve. I had the same operation in London at almost exactly the same age. When he was well enough, he was shipped to San Francisco, where he passed the remainder of the war administering dental care on a navy base in the mornings and playing golf in the afternoons for free on some of the best courses in the western United States. Most American courses were made available to military personnel throughout the duration of the war. He remembered with some dismay carloads of uniformed servicemen driving past a course where he was playing and shouting out "Slackers!" at him and his playing partners, believing them to have avoided military service.

I can no more remember first becoming aware of golf than first becoming aware of eating, for in spite of my father's efforts at temperance with respect to the sport, golf seemed lodged in our home like another family member that had been born unassisted and ectoplasmically out of him. The angels on his trophies looked down at us from the top of a cupboard as we ate. In the evenings sometimes when I did my homework, I could hear the faint click of ball on club as he practiced his putting on the strip of carpet that led from my bedroom to the room with the television at the back of our apartment. It was in that room that I sat with him to watch *Shell's Wonderful World of Golf* or the final rounds of tournaments. I remember him getting dressed in his golf clothes and saying good-bye to my mother and me on weekend mornings before driving out to the airbase course for matches. It seemed so grand and fascinating and gladiatorial, part of an adult world I could never imagine inhabiting. As the time drew near for him to return, I'd watch the clock, anxious to hear his news. Even the seasons took much of their definition from golf and the manner in which he played it—there were his rain-splattered windbreaker hanging on a hook in the kitchen after an early-spring round, the trips by boat to the golf course from that same house on the Wisconsin lake where his friend had awakened to find him practicing a one-armed swing and where we came to spend our summer holidays, the ritual autumn polishing of his golf shoes and the cleaning with brush and nail file of his clubs before they were put away for the winter. They then sat in a closet from October to the following April, inanimate yet somehow on the verge of life, like dolls in a fairy story.

There is a photograph of me taken in a park when I was around two years old holding a golf club in a proprietorial manner. But I did not begin to play then. By some standards I began late, when I was eight. I was going one evening with my father and mother to have dinner somewhere and we stopped at a driving range on the way so that he could hit a bucket of balls. Evidently I interrupted him and asked if I could hit a few myself, and he agreed. He had done nothing that evening or at any previous time to bring the game to me because he thought it better that I find my own way to it. He was the same many years later with dentistry. He thought it could be a possible profession for me and, with the idea of introducing me to it, had invited me to his office on a Friday night, the day of the week he stayed late to do his laboratory work. Afterward we were to go to dinner. I was around seventeen at the time. When I arrived, he took me into his laboratory and showed me a bridge he was working on and began to explain how he would go about completing it. "That's fine," I said, interrupting him, "I'll wait for you outside," and then went into his waiting room to read. I had no idea

of what was at stake for him in this moment. He finally told me about it, with some amusement, more than twenty years later.

My reaction to golf was the antithesis of my reaction to dentistry. I went to driving ranges with him and took up a position on the mat beside his with my own bucket of balls. I practiced putting on the same strip of carpet where he practiced. I broke the glass top of a table swinging a seven iron in the living room. I went along with him and my mother on holiday rounds and was allowed to hit a few shots from time to time. Eventually I was given a set of my mother's clubs and began to play whole rounds. As a teacher he was simple, classical, knowledgeable. Square setup, overlapping Vardon grip, turn on a central axis with the head still, smooth tempo. "You can't overpower a golf shot," he said. Once when I ran loudly down some stairs, he told me I should move fluidly, with my knees. "Heavyweight boxers wouldn't crash down the stairs like that. They'd be silent. Strength is something graceful. Look at golf. Some of the longest hitters look like they're making almost no effort at all."

Then there were those allegorical injunctions—"Commit yourself to the shot," "Don't give up on it," "Smooth acceleration from the top of the backswing," "Keep your head down," "Follow through." You can see the reasons for such instructions by looking at poor players, particularly from a distance. Their swings are short and fast and nervous. They bring the club around their bodies from outside to in rather than extending their arms outward on the follow-through. Their nervousness and haste increase as they approach the top of the backswing and then they lunge at the ball with a kind of hysterical slap, their weight falling onto the back foot. This is due to fear and impatience and a sense of losing a control they do not possess. They look up before completing their swings because of their anxiety to see where the ball is going. They set up with open stances for the same reason. The entire movement appears to be going backward as though contact with the ball will scald them. It is all nervousness, timidity, fear of failure. A good golf shot from such a swing as this is merely a matter of luck.

A good golf swing seen from a distance on the other hand looks smooth, slow, long, well-balanced, and controlled. This comes from hitting thousands upon thousands of shots. But in the fullness of the backswing and of the extension of the arms as they move into and through the ball, the head kept down and back as the body advances and turns, there must be an element of faith in oneself as the body enters the hitting area and then releases itself into the unknown. You need those things my father spoke about to get through this—a solid base, a movement beyond where your fears would like you to stop, then a kind of controlled abandon. But in retrospect, there seems more that can be taken from those admonishments than just tips for golf, spoken as they were from father to son.

Most of my golf for the first few years was played at a nine-hole course near the Wisconsin lake where my father's friend had his house. I usually played with my mother and her women friends while my father played with the men. I played with my mother one summer afternoon in front of a man who hole after hole hit his tee shots before we were out of range. None had hit us but some had come quite close. We couldn't let him through because another

group was immediately ahead of us. My mother called out to him
to be more careful, but the bombardment continued. Finally we
reached the last hole. My mother and I had hit our drives into a hol-
low visible from the tee only through a periscope and were waiting
to hit our second shots when my father walked out to meet us, having just finished his match. He asked us how we were doing. We
said we were doing all right but that the man behind us had been
hitting into us throughout the round. Just then a ball came over the
hill and whistled past me two inches from my nose. I felt a rush of
air and then saw the ball bounding along the fairway ahead of us.
"Did you say you asked him not to do that?" my father asked my
mother. "Yes," she said. "Several times." He looked back toward
the tee to gauge the distance and took a three wood from my bag.
He walked over to the man's ball then and hit it directly back at him.
His woods and long irons had a wonderful shape to them that
I have never been able to attain—starting low to the ground, then
rising and drawing, rather like Arnold Palmer's. He hit this one
beautifully, as shots struck in anger sometimes are. I watched the
ball sail over the hill and imagined it crashing into one of the upper
branches of the high trees around the tee and then dropping onto
the man's head just as he was returning his driver to his bag.

None of my neighborhood friends played golf, until the Dore
brothers took it up. The Dore brothers were good students and
superb athletes and after conquering all around them in the con-
ventional sports had set up a one-hole golf course at the school
playground. This playground was an asphalted rectangle containing three basketball nets and was bordered on two sides by streets,

one side by the convent housing the nuns who taught us, and finally the last side by the backs of houses. The hole laid out by the Dores began with a tee set up in the grass adjacent to one of the streets, traversed the short part of the playground, narrowed to just a few feet as it passed through the gate to their house, and ended in a hole that they had dug in their backyard. They knew of my interest in golf and invited me to play their hole. The tee shot now would be half a wedge for me, but we all used drivers. I hit a low line drive that passed through the gaps in the fence of their neighbors' house to the right, flipped a wedge from their lawn into the Dores' yard, and then two-putted for a four. This, the Dores told me, was the course record, the only one I will surely ever hold and one that has not been broken, for the course was closed that afternoon due to complaints from neighbors.

My contemporaries moved collectively into golf when we reached the age when we could begin caddying. We caddied at the Edgewater Golf Club, a private club with wealthy members and tight fairways that was set down in an urban neighborhood. If you hit a bad slice on any of the first five holes, your ball could end up in a drive-in restaurant, a used-car lot, or someone's bedroom. The club closed in the early 1970s and there is now a city park with a small nine-hole course on the land, but Edgewater lives in a small corner of the history of golf because it was the home course of the legendary Chick Evans, winner of three major championships, as well as numerous other tournaments, in the early part of the twentieth century. Some would say that from tee to green he was the best of his time, but he remained an amateur. He simply couldn't picture himself as a pro, he explained. As a child he had caddied at Edge-water and he maintained a relationship with the club throughout his life. He was much sought after as a caddy because he found balls others couldn't by lying flat on the ground and then rotating himself like a rolling pin through the rough. Years later he set up a scholarship foundation, which has sent hundreds of caddies to college. By the time I knew him he was an elderly, perpetually smiling man with a propensity for poetic flights of language. My father was his dentist and also played quite a lot of golf with him. I have a letter to my father from Chick praising his dental skills and his golf swing in a single lyrical and rapturous sentence.

I worked at Edgewater for six summers from when I was thirteen until I entered university, and it formed the setting for a rite of passage for me perhaps like what running away with the circus was for an earlier generation. As I was to discover again later, and contrary to received beliefs, the world of golf has a highly varied populace, perhaps more highly varied than other subsections of society. I met people at Edgewater I would almost certainly never otherwise have met. I met churchmen and pillars of the bourgeoisie. I met mafiosi, alcoholics, bankrupts, teenage gang members, millionaires, Mexican guitar players, movie stars, professional gamblers, gigolos, and aspiring pros. I used to play with one of those aspiring pros, a fine player named Denny Lavin, whom Chick Evans had taken a particular interest in and who many believed would have a chance on the tour, until these ambitions were rapidly dissolved in an early marriage, fatherhood, and a job in a factory.

An itinerant band of professional caddies were allowed to work on the course in spring and autumn when schoolboy caddies were scarce. They were for the most part alcoholics, wanderers, men who could find no permanent place into which they could fit. They sat under the trees near the caddy shack and drank cheap sherry out of paper bags. They all seemed to have nicknames. I remember one in particular, a tall, haunted-looking man called Al the Eye because of a large, empurpled deformity in that part of his face. If you paid them, they'd buy you beer.

Up to that time my knowledge of sex was limited to what I could gather from very often misconceived playground badinage and one dour, dispiriting lecture with anatomical charts given us by one of the parish priests. At Edgewater I met it everywhere. I saw a friend of my mother's whose husband was away arriving at the club one evening with a bachelor member in his convertible Cadillac. She was laughing, the wind was blowing through her hair. She had on a little dress with polka dots. When she saw me, her eyes widened and she blushed. When she said hello to me, she stammered. She later became very religious and I wondered if that moment had anything to do with it. I heard a rumor, elaborated by locker-room attendants, that a member had drunkenly tried to mount an inflatable doll with simulated parts in a small sleeping room. He'd left the door ajar, apparently. Every morning I had breakfast with a lesbian named Jamie, the locker-room cook. She lifted weights, rolled her packet of Lucky Strike cigarettes in the sleeve of her T-shirt, and lived in a trailer behind the fourteenth green with a long-legged, languorous, spectacularly beautiful waitress whose shape could give you vertigo. One of the Mexican greenskeepers made a pass at her and Jamie hit him so hard that he went rolling backward down the kitchen stairs all the way to the cellar. One sunny morning a fellow caddy and I sat in the grass by the tee as we waited for our group to hit their drives and he told me about the powerful effect you could produce in girls by licking between their toes. "That's what they like more than anything," he told me. For the members, we were often invisible, so we overheard many details of their lives, financial, domestic, sexual. I remember Jim Flanagan, a tall, long-hitting Southerner with a two handicap, fitting on a new golf glove, running his fingers over the leather palm and saying, "As smooth as the inside of a schoolteacher's thigh." That seemed then, as it does now, astonishingly precise and privileged information.

The actor Martin Sheen once worked as a caddy and said that the experience taught him at an early age how ugly is the exercise of privilege. Caddies are like barmen in their quick acquisition of a jaded sense of humor due to repeated close observation of foibles and grotesqueries, particularly of the rich and powerful, while remaining unobserved themselves. There is a joke about a rich and boorish American playing in Scotland who blasphemes and throws clubs as he tops, shanks, and slices his way around the course before finally turning to his caddy after a missed putt and exploding, "You are absolutely the worst caddy this game has ever seen!" The caddy takes a draw on his cigarette. "Oh, no, sir," he says. "That would be too much of a coincidence."

At Edgewater we sat around the caddy shack trying to outdo each other in our imitations of the idiocy of the members. We had a particular aversion to members who addressed us as "son." The only ones excluded from this were a group known to us as The Boys, seven or eight low-handicappers who played every day at around eleven o'clock for high stakes. We were in awe of them. We were in awe of them because they played for such large amounts of money, they were good golfers, and they tipped better than anyone else. They played a game with six possible points available on each hole, starting at $20 per point, rising through repeated pressings, or doublings, until the stakes reached $320 per point or more, a significant sum in the 1960s. This was compounded by side bets. These men had businesses that evidently needed little scrutiny from them. One sold perfume, another provided security guards. Jim Flanagan published a racing sheet. But there was one, Jack McGrath, whose only apparent income was from gambling at golf and cards at the club. He had a wife and at least one child, membership fees, and living expenses to deal with and played off a five handicap, which he couldn't inflate because he played every day with the same people. He fascinated me. I couldn't imagine how he could do it. He must, I thought, be living with perpetually frayed nerves.

One of the members on the periphery of this group was a thirteen-handicapper named Mickey Mason, who once went out and played another member for $1,000 per hole. He was bald and smoked fat cigars and boasted that he was the only Jew to evade the scrutiny of this racially exclusionary club. He had a regular caddy named Moose O'Brien, who was immense and terrifying and used to surreptitiously roll the ball in the rough to improve the lie, though with or without his employer's knowledge I cannot say. Moose told us about going to a hooker and paying I believe $20 for an initial session and then $10 each for two more "positions." I tried for a long time to imagine what he meant by this.

Long after the club had closed and the members had dispersed and I had gone to live on another continent, I heard a story about Mickey Mason from a former Edgewater member who was a friend of my father's. Mason borrowed money from a gangster, and when he couldn't make the payment at the appointed time, the gangster organized the kidnapping of Mason's only child. I'd seen this boy once at a rest stop on a highway when I was on vacation with my parents and he with his. He was blond and handsome and seemed rather delicate and had arrived in Mason's life when he was in his forties. The money was found and the boy was released. Mason then went to a golf course where he knew the gangster was playing. He found him out on the back nine somewhere waiting for his turn to putt. He walked up onto the green, pointed a gun at the man, and said, "That's the last time you fuck with my family." Then he shot him dead.

I saw Bob Hope play at Edgewater and one of the men out of Peter, Paul, and Mary, but far more impressive to me was Marty Stanovitch, the legendary hustler known in that beyond-the-frontier world of gamblers as the Fat Man. He played cards, and I believe shot a little pool, but most of his income came from golf. He played big-money games all around the country with players who knew all about him, including, I was to learn later, Arnold Palmer, but mostly he worked the resorts, applying Pan-Cake makeup in the mornings to disguise his tan and pass himself off as a newly arrived tourist. He might work on one person for more than a week, losing a couple of times and perhaps narrowly winning before moving in for the payoff. Once he had his fingers broken on the West Coast.

He came to Edgewater when I was around sixteen to play a money match with The Boys. I went out to the first tee to look at him. He was a short, round man with sparse strands of greased-back hair and a pencil mustache. In my memory he looks a little like the corrupt grandee in Orson Welles's *Touch of Evil.* He kept his swing short and flat to get it around his high, tight stomach, and also, perhaps, to make it look unthreatening. He had a worn canvas bag stained with what looked like car grease. Both woods and irons were old, battered, and mismatched. One of the irons had perforations in the face instead of grooves and an antique steel shaft painted a streaked brown to make it look like hickory. The whipping was coming loose around the neck of his driver. His clubs looked just as they were meant to look—as if they had been bought in a yard sale. Had I not known who he was, I would have felt confident of beating him.

A few hours later I watched him come up the eighteenth hole. It was a par four that doglegged left, and he had hit his drive beyond a line of trees to the right. About 160 yards remained to the green, and he had not only to hit the shot with a steep trajectory but also to draw it around the trees, just clear a bunker tight to the right-hand front of the green, and stop the ball quickly. I heard the distant click of the club striking the ball and then saw it drop like a feather, twelve feet from the hole.

When I saw him in the clubhouse, I asked him how he had played.

"I did lousy," he said, spreading his hands in a gesture of self-accusation. "Sixty-nine."

Many years later in a Park Lane hotel in London I heard a story about Marty Stanovitch from Barbara Romack, one of the leading American women professionals from the 1960s. She was on a brief European tour with a friend of my mother's. She asked me if I knew where she could find the best casinos in London and displayed an animated interest in gambling, something that is perhaps not uncommon in high-level athletes. I asked her if she knew Marty Stanovitch. She did, she said. During the off-season she toured with him sometimes looking for money matches in the South and West. She told me that one day they were playing a match in California, and as they were walking up the eighteenth fairway, a young black man ran out from the clubhouse to meet them.

"Can we play tomorrow, Mr. Stanovitch?" he asked.

"Sure."

"Same time, same bet?"

"That's fine. I'll see you on the first tee at nine o'clock."

The young man ran back to where he had come from.

"Who's he?" asked Barbara.

"He's a guy I've been playing with out here the last couple of years. He's got a lot of talent. But he'll never beat me."

"Why's that?"

"He's strong, he hits the ball real good. But always with a draw.

Even a nine iron he draws. So what I do is, I get up early and give the greenskeeper fifty bucks to cut all the pins front right. The poor guy can never get the ball near the hole. He just can't figure out what goes wrong."

When later I was writing something about professional gamblers, I wanted to include these men who ranged the open road with their golf bags in the trunks of their cars, improvising, using their imaginations, looking for that finely calibrated edge, entertaining themselves and others as they preyed on human greed with their feats of leverage and deception. I called Barbara Romack in Florida to ask where they were. "They're gone," she said. "Extinct."

All schoolboy caddies started at the bottom, carrying for women Tuesday mornings and low-tipping hackers the rest of the time. The best bags went to older and bigger boys. Of these I remember a shaven-headed athlete named John Carney and a mountainous character named Fish, who was notorious all over the north side of Chicago for his ability to maim people in brawls. John Carney once arranged the purchase of several quarts of beer for a group of friends of mine and me when my parents were away overnight. We were out all day watching a practice round of the Western Open and hadn't eaten anything before starting to drink the beer at my house in the early evening. Apart from a small sip of my father's bourbon, I'd never drunk alcohol before. I was sixteen at the time. I remember stumbling through our apartment over collapsed bodies to get to the bathroom, which was full of beer bottles. I looked long and searchingly in the mirror. I couldn't find a way of connecting myself to the face I saw looking back at me. Shortly after that

I passed out. John Carney laughed at me the next day when I showed up at the club, pale and trembling. That I had nothing to compare to the state I found myself in increased its awfulness. I could not smell or even contemplate beer for the succeeding five years. As for Fish, he left caddying after finishing high school and became a policeman, like others I knew in Chicago given to the practice of beating people up at weekends. I remember coming out of an elevated train station and seeing him in uniform standing by the door. He told me about all the fun he'd had beating up demonstrators at the Chicago Democratic Convention that summer of 1968. He was fearsome, but surprisingly, I thought, friendly and solicitous toward me.

I hung on as a caddy while a number of my friends went on to summer jobs as camp counselors or construction workers or waiters. I ascended through the ranks due to their absence, my regular attendance, and my marginally superior knowledge of golf. Eventually I became the regular caddy of one of The Boys, Bob Kane, a wild and very long eight-handicapper with the strongest grip I'd ever seen, the V's formed by thumb and forefinger improbably pointing to somewhere below his right elbow. His son, then in his twenties, was also a big hitter. I remember him coming out of the clubhouse from a dinner one evening in shirt and tie and dress shoes and knocking a ball through the fading light onto the first green, 358 yards away. I liked Bob Kane very much, and I got to see at close range good players in tense matches for high stakes, but when I was offered a full-time summer job cleaning clubs and putting on new grips in the bag room, I took it. The following summer

I became assistant to the starter, a small, diabetic Scots former professional named Charlie Pairman, who was terse and punctilious and whom I admired greatly. He embodied something about golf I had not seen before, something to do with his silence and gravity. Perhaps it was his Scottishness. These jobs provided me with my first regular paychecks. They also gave me access to the course. I could play all day on Mondays and each evening after the last of the members had gone out. The evenings I came to see as my time, the day's work finished, family and other involvements of the night not yet begun, when I would go out alone with the air cooling and the sun low and the sound of birdsong and the whack of club on ball echoing in the tree-lined fairways. A golf course still looks its most inviting to me at this time of day. I often tried to get Charlie to come out with me when we finished work, but he would never do it. He had turned his back on golf, at least on the playing of it. That was a mystery to me and still is whenever I hear of others doing it.

Golf had by my midteenage years assumed an imperial presence in my life. I read instruction books and golf magazines. I kept my sand wedge under the desk in the starter's office, and whenever I could, I hit shots from the bunker in front of the ninth green. During afternoons in the school year when the weather was good, I hit hundreds of nine-iron shots on a football field near our home. I had a yearning to see the thrilling high-arcing shape of golf shots everywhere—out of classroom windows, along highways, from the tops of buildings. One afternoon I was waiting for a train after a round at a lakeside public course called Waveland. The Chicago Cubs baseball park, Wrigley Field, was adjacent to the station. There

Charlie Pairman *(left)* with Timothy O'Grady.
(Photo courtesy of the author.)

was no one around. I took out a four wood, teed up a ball between the wooden slats of the platform, and hit it cleanly over the billboards and apartment building rooftops and into the baseball park. At night in my bed in those years I played heroic rounds in my mind before going to sleep. I talked about golf incessantly. It felt sometimes like something I could not quite contain, like something from which I needed some relief.

On the larger stage of golf at that time two of the greatest players in the history of the game, Jack Nicklaus and Arnold Palmer, were battling for supremacy. The presence of Palmer in particular gave another dimension to many people's personal obsessions with the game—certainly to mine. Whether he won or lost, and how he did it, had an urgency and importance that I did not feel again until I watched Muhammad Ali fight Joe Frazier and George Foreman in the following decade. Palmer seemed so different from the others, with their careful calculations, their masks of imperturbability, their smaller anxieties. He charged putts at the hole from fifty feet and beyond and crashed his driver off the fairway to water-encircled greens 280 yards away. His swing was a wild, ungainly, muscular explosion that almost no one could understand. Gary Player said that when he first saw Palmer hitting balls, sparks seemed to fly up from the grass. You could see everything that was happening inside him in his face, the anguish and the glories. It was like violently changing weather patterns. He played golf of the possible, however remote, rather than the probable. He was often to be found deep in a wood, grass and twigs flying up around him and his torso bobbing like a middleweight's as he strained to follow the flight of his ball through a tiny aperture in the branches of a tree up ahead. Everyone watching him seemed as anxious and expectant as he did. "Arnold would never protect a lead," said Lee Trevino. "He just kept firing for birdies. He'd go for the flag off an alligator's back." At Augusta in 1964 he arrived at the par five fifteenth on the final day with a lead over the field of five shots. After his drive he faced a long second shot to a shallow green protected by water at the front. Probably every other player in the tournament, if in his position, would have hit an iron safely short of the water. He took his three wood and swung at the ball with tremendous force. As it sailed toward the green, he lost sight of it in the afternoon sun. "Did it get over?" he asked his playing partner, Dave Marr. "Arnold," drawled Marr, "your *divot* got over."

I was too young to appreciate him during his best years, the stretch of 1958–64 when he won his seven major titles. By the time the mania truly had me in its thrall, Nicklaus had more or less won the battle. But Palmer remained a threatening and compelling figure. He generated an energy in the game generally that people hacking away on courses all over the world could feel the effect of. As reading great literature can make you want to write, so watching Arnold Palmer made you want to play golf.

Those regular summer-evening few holes I played at Edgewater provided me with a middling ability. When I was seventeen and eighteen, I was playing off nine, or perhaps ten, while harboring the illusion that my true game, the game that was inside me, was in fact much better than that. If only I had time to practice more, if only I got some good breaks, if only I could sort out the ridiculous and tedious business of chipping and putting, then, surely, I would play to my true potential. This is an illusion I have not ceased to chase, though at least I no longer believe chipping and putting to be ridiculous. I was on, then off, and then finally again on my high school golf team. In the Chicago Catholic League finals I shot eighty-two after hitting fourteen greens in regulation. The round included forty-two putts. Had I taken two putts per hole—which is not too much to ask, I told myself—I would have shot a four-over-par seventy-six and been one behind the low gross scorer for the day. Also, our team would have won the championship. My score that day seemed more an irrationality or bad luck or plague than flawed playing. Putting was something I thought extraneous to good golf. In some adolescent way I may even have been proud that my sound tee-to-green play had been undone by this fiddly activity at which even elderly ladies can excel. It certainly did not occur to me that I should learn more about this part of the game, and practice it.

I have never again played as much golf as I did in those years, but I only rarely played with my father. He had his playing companions and I had mine. We talked quite a lot about golf, however, and I was always interested in learning about his rounds. I remember the pleasure I had listening to his story about being drawn against a notorious cheat in his club's Class A Championship. Whenever he tried to fix a time to play the match, the other man declared himself busy. Finally the man suggested that they play separately and match scorecards later. For years my father had watched him collect trophies that were not rightly his. "If I have to play you at midnight with a flashlight, I will do it," said my father. On the day that they played the match my father hooked his drive on the second hole and the ball came to rest against the trunk of a tree. He played it back out into the fairway left-handed using the reverse side of his putter. "I'm afraid that's a two-stroke penalty as turning the putter around makes an extra club in your bag and that puts you over the limit," said his opponent. This is incorrect, of course, as my father knew, but to be called a rule-breaker by a cheat and then magisterially absolved was more than was tolerable to him. He bore down and won the match six and five. "It's best to play with a controlled mad," said Sam Snead.

But about matters other than golf I was beginning to test the relationship, to goad him and push him toward and perhaps beyond his limits. At dinner I would summon whatever vituperative language I then had and in long monologues assault the hypocrisy of the Catholic Church, the immorality of American policy in Vietnam, the corruption of the bourgeoisie. He never quite took the bait. At times he agreed, at other times he held his ground. But he never lost his temper, though he must surely occasionally have found it wearisome. This is adolescence, this is, I suppose, the Oedipus complex, that psychological disposition that Freud thought the most deeply embedded of all. The son craves the admiration of the father, but he also strives to surpass him, and in some figurative way to kill him.

We were fortunate, I think, to have golf to absorb some of this, to provide an arena in which the drama could play or at least talk some part of itself out. Most fathers and sons did not have this, for most did not share an activity in which they could compete as equals. Just after I graduated from high school and a few weeks before I fell in love with Ruth Farrell, my father offered me a round of golf as a graduation present. I think it was the first round we would play together during that summer in which golf was to recede from its place of importance in my life. I was playing well, for me. I wanted him to see what I could do—particularly at the venue he had chosen, for it was heavy with symbolism. We were to play all twenty-seven holes at the Butterfield Country Club, the course on which he had probably played his most enjoyable and best golf and toward which he had felt compelled to turn his back upon my arrival in his life.

It was a still, sunny June day. We had lockers assigned to us and had lunch in the men's locker room. Various members and employees came over to greet him. I saw his name engraved on plaques as the winner of various competitions. We went out to the first tee. We were to play a warm-up nine and then proceed to the official eighteen. As at all private clubs, we were compelled to take a caddy, a great embarrassment to me as I had so recently been a caddy myself. I walked next to him and talked to him throughout the round in case I might be taken as the visitor's equivalent of a member's son, that human subspecies about whom the Edgewater caddies had been at their most corrosive. I don't remember much about the round, except a few sunlit images and the fact that I played solidly and avoided falling apart at any point. I had a thirty-nine on, I think, the second nine we played and an eighty or eighty-one over the eighteen. This was two shots or so better than my father. I also had the better score over the entire twenty-seven holes. I had beaten him. This had never happened before.

After I added up the scorecard I turned to him and said, "I won."

He looked down at his shoes until he found a reply, then looked again at me.

"It's about time," he said finally.

Indeed it was. He was sixty-three and I was eighteen. Yet this made it no easier for him entirely to accept.

Not long after that round at Butterfield it all faded away, for then came Ruth Farrell, protest marches, cross-country hitchhiking, visionary literature, wine, music, and rhapsodic talk through the night, and golf for a time became a small, nearly forgotten thing in my life.

3

·

Can Golf Save the World?

No civilization had as profound a belief in the importance of sport as the ancient Greeks, but they did not invent golf. The pharaoh Tuthmosis III hit leather spheres stuffed with wool and clay into the desert with a club carved from olive wood, and the Romans played a game called *paganica* in which a feather-stuffed ball was batted down a street toward the opposition's goal, but neither of these activities could be described as golf. The invention of golf was evidently begun around 1300 in Holland as a game played with sticks and balls on frozen canals, the aim of which was to hit a stake embedded in the ice, and completed around 150 years later by Scotsmen who added the defining presence of the hole. These holes were originally rabbit scrapes dug in sandy grassland near the sea and marked by gulls' feathers. No one knows for certain how the game moved from Holland to Scotland. Some say it was Scottish wool merchants delayed in Holland by poor weather and introduced to what the Dutch called *kolf* by hospitable clients. Nor is it known why it was transformed into a game with a hole. But by 1457 there was already enough of a mania around it for the Scottish parliament to declare that "the Fute-ball and Golfe be utterly cryit doune, and nocht usit." It seems that these two games were interfering with soldiers practicing their archery.

There has long been a connection between golf and the military, from those earliest days to the founding in 1829 of the first golf club outside Scotland, the Dum Dum in Calcutta, by a Scots regiment stationed there, to the continued influential presence in golf of military men, particularly those austere and fastidious ex-officers who when retired go in for freelance proofreading and club secretaryships. It was soldiers with time on their hands who built the first courses in continental Europe and Africa. Captain Alan Shepard took golf to the moon.

There is a record of Musselburgh, Scotland, fishwives playing in competition in 1810, which indicates an early democratizing presence in the game. But golf was expensive. Balls imported into Scotland from Holland cost so much that the Stuart court established an official ballmaker to undercut them. The balls in use for golf 's first four hundred years were called featheries, and it took one man an entire day to make two of them, each fashioned from two top hats full of boiled goose feathers and a leather pouch. Monarchs played it, particularly Scots. James I was a fanatic who overrode the

Church's objections to golf being played on Sundays. Mary, Queen of Scots, is said to have played golf days after Darnley's murder as a public display of her indifference. Charles I was on a course at Leith when he first learned of an insurrection in Ireland. James II played a big-money match against two English noblemen with a poor shoemaker named John Patersone as his partner, and Patersone won enough that day to build a new house.

Why Scotland? Is a nation expressed in its games? I don't know that country well enough to say, but Arnold Haultain advances a theory. "Golf," he says, "is self-reliant, silent, sturdy. It leans less on its fellows. It loves best to overcome obstacles alone. . . . There is something Puritanically and Sinaitically threatening in the thought of 'approaching' a hole; as if, puir aperture, it were not to be come at but after due preparation thereunto, and were altogether fenced off from the ignorant, the scandalous and the profane." I suppose there is a severity to those gray Scottish skies and that even grayer Edinburgh stone, to the unadorned Calvanist churches and the messages handed down from their pulpits, just as there is a severity to golf. There is no absolution in golf, whereas football, billiards, tennis, and baseball, along with numerous other sports, constantly present the competitor with another chance. In golf you can blow a four-day stroke-play tournament with a single errant shot. And in golf you stand alone, and exposed. There is no team in which to hide. But I think golf as a precise cultural or religious metaphor is an unsustainable idea. There are too many Catholics, for example, playing it well. Tiger Woods is in part a Thai Buddhist.

Having been moribund since the ancient Greek games, organized sport exploded suddenly and spectacularly in Western society in the mid-nineteenth century, particularly in Britain. As the Caribbean writer C.L.R. James says in his great book about cricket, *Beyond a Boundary*, "Golf was known to be ancient, but the first tournament of the Open championship was held only in 1860." He then points out that the Football Association was founded in 1863, the first modern athletics championship was held in England in 1866, the first English cricket team left for Australia in 1862, and the first professional baseball team was put together in the United States in 1869. This was of course a time of mass industrialization, of the mechanization of agriculture, and of the great expansion of cities, with their populace's need for organized diversion and vicarious physicality. As the hockey player Eric Nesterenko explains in *Working*, Studs Terkel's epochal record of work in America, "Being a physical man in the modern world is becoming obsolete—the machines have taken the place of that. We work in offices, we fight rules and corporations, but we hardly ever hit anybody. Not that hitting anybody is a solution. But to survive in the world at one time, one had to stand up and fight—fight the weather, fight the land, or fight the rocks. I think there is a real desire for man to do that. Today he has evolved into being more passive, conforming . . . I think that is why the professional game, with its terrific physicality—men getting together on a cooperative basis—this is appealing to the middle-class man. He is the one who supports professional sports." It is perhaps for these reasons that professional sport has risen in importance in proportion to the growth of cities. Golf, of course, is neither as cooperative or physical as hockey, but it has its own manner of displaying combat, poise, valor, raw nerve, and physical mastery.

C.L.R. James saw something more in the coincidence of so many sports being organized and rising to prominence in a single decade of the nineteenth century. "Disraeli's Reform Bill, introducing popular democracy in England, was passed in 1865. In the same year the slave states were defeated in the American Civil War, to be followed immediately by the first modern organization of American labor. In 1864 Karl Marx and Frederick Engels founded the first Communist International and within a few years Europe for the first time since the Crusades saw an international organization comprising millions of people. In 1871 in France Napoleon III was overthrown and the Paris Commune was established. . . . So that this same public that wanted sports and games so eagerly wanted popular democracy too. Perhaps they were not the same people in each case. Even so, both groups were stirred at the same time." Intellectuals from Matthew Arnold to Trotsky dismissed sport as a trifle or a distraction. They could not see it as a form of self-expression nor understand people's need to bear witness to it. They could not see it as Solon did when he answered a barbarian's question about the Greeks' obsession with sport by saying, "I cannot find words to give you an idea of the pleasure that you would have if you were seated in the middle of the anxious spectators, watching the courage of the athletes, the beauty of their bodies, their splendid poses, their extraordinary suppleness, their tireless energy, their audacity, their sense of competition . . . their unceasing efforts to win a victory. I am sure you would not cease to overwhelm them with praise, to shout again and again, to applaud." Forty thousand people used to gather in Athens for the original Olympics. Plato and Pythagoras always sat in the front row. Even Diogenes, the founder of Cynicism, who dressed in rags and carried a candle as he looked for an honest man, came to the games.

In addition to these social and political considerations, there was a technological factor in the opening out of golf to the masses—the introduction of the gutta-percha ball in 1848. Gutta-percha is a gumlike substance emitted from tropical trees that acts like a thermoplastic—that is, it can be molded when hot and hardens when cool. There is a legend that the Reverend R. Patterson invented the gutta-percha ball after receiving a statue of the Hindu god Vishnu from his half brother, a missionary in India. The statue was packed in gutta-percha chips, some of which fell into the Reverend Patterson's fire as he opened the package. He watched the chips melt in the heat, then rolled some of the resulting mass into a ball. As it cooled, it hardened. He was struck by its resemblance to a golf ball and decided to take it out on the course to hit a few shots with it. He found that after the ball acquired the nicks and scratches it needed to get airborne, it flew beautifully, considerably farther than a featherie. It would also be more durable and far cheaper to produce. It could be mass-produced in a factory rather than handmade in a pro shop. The legend is almost certainly false, but what is known definitely is that while the gutta-percha ball was resisted by most professionals as both untraditional and threatening to their livelihoods, it was enthused over by Old Tom Morris, then an assistant pro at

St. Andrews but eventually as dominant a figure in golf as was W. G. Grace in cricket.

Intrepid, entrepreneurial, and games-loving Scots, along with a few Englishmen, took the game out into the world. Courses were built in South Africa, Canada, and Australia, usually commissioned by a Scots army officer or millionaire and then staffed by Scots teaching professionals and clubmakers. Golf grew steadily in these English-speaking imperial outposts. It took some time to settle in the United States. Three Dutchmen were fined in Albany, New York, in 1657 for playing their version of the game on ice on a Sunday. "Veritable Canadian balls" were offered on sale in New York City in 1799, and there were perhaps courses of some description in Savannah, Georgia, and Charleston, South Carolina, as early as 1788 and 1811 respectively, but they faded away, as did another attempt to establish a club near White Sulphur Springs, West Virginia, in 1884. Golf was finally established in the United States by John Reid, a Scot from Dunfermline who grew rich operating an ironworks in Yonkers, New York. He had never played golf, but he had an enthusiasm for games and asked a friend named Robert Lockhart visiting Scotland to bring him back some supplies. Lockhart bought a set of clubs and two dozen gutta-percha balls at Old Tom Morris's pro shop, and Reid later tried them out on an improvised three-hole course in a cow pasture on a prematurely warm day in February 1888. Later that year Reid, Lockhart, and a few friends who came collectively to be known as The Apple Tree Gang convened and founded the first lasting golf club in the United States, which they named St. Andrews.

Since then golf has exploded sensationally. It has for some time been the world's fastest-growing sport. It can be played in all seriousness by infants and geriatrics and every age in between. The one-armed, the blind, and the wheelchair-bound play golf. Hackers and scratch players can compete on equal terms through the handicap system. Mass-manufacture and the proliferation of cheap public courses run by municipalities have brought the game within reach of virtually anyone with a job. Many young men who might otherwise have thought that their experience of sport had ended with school are now taking up golf in exponentially increasing numbers. Thousands of retired people elect to fill the long days of their latter years with the game and move to places with sunny climates specifically so that they can play it every day. Golf is an enormous, ever-expanding business, important in real estate development, the media, corporate self-promotion, and tourism. Golf courses are being built all around the world and there are now university degree courses in greenkeeping. Club and ball manufacturers are divisions of international conglomerates, at one end of which are the appetites of the shareholders and at the other those of the consumers.

In between is the industry itself. Central to it are the engineers who apply evolving ideas in aerodynamics to balls and test new metals and thermoplastics, lighter and with higher ballistic capacities, for clubs. Many of these substances have been developed by the aerospace industry and have arrived at the club-manufacturing plants through scientific journals and university physics and engineering departments. Prototypes are cast, the workers on the factory

floor guide them through the multitudinous stages of manufactur-
ing, robots and professionals test them, ads are placed, brochures
written in a promotional language of breakthrough, discovery, and
the promise of invincibility are distributed, and marketing men
and sales representatives go out by car and plane to try to sell
them, the whole system struggling to prey on the illusion that golf
is conquerable. Professionals are paid $1 million or more a year to
have the names of these manufacturers stitched onto the sides of
their bags. Golf began with hedgethorn and briar, then moved
on to apple, pear, and beech wood. Drop-forged iron increased
the spectrum of shot-making. Everything was handmade. Now
ever-hopeful golfers can approach the first tee with precision-
matched, perimeter-weighted, beryllium-copper, square-grooved
irons with low torque, low kick-point, and a neutralizer hosel,
carbon-graphite woods with titanium, boron-reinforced shafts, a
thermoplastically crafted driver adapted from bulletproof vests,
pump-action shoes, a spiral octahelix dimple-patterned ball with
extrafine urethane cover, and a putter that looks like an obscure
piece of plumbing.

Golf was once exclusively confined to the English-speaking
world. It is now global. The golf industry traverses the world in
search of new markets. Japan, Sweden, and Argentina have been
cultivated for decades, but much of the rest of the world is there to
be worked. In Southeast Asia and the Pacific, China, Russia, and
Central Europe, there are new bourgeoisies being created who
might be persuaded to see golf as a leisure activity that confers status on the participant. These countries will also, of course, spawn

their own genuine addicts interested in the game solely for what it, as a sport, or fascination, can offer, or take.

Professional golf experienced two great leaps forward in the money made available to it and the status accorded it—first, in the 1920s, because of Walter Hagen, and then in the 1960s because of Arnold Palmer. These men had great victories, great fame, great marketability. Professional golf has now entered a new epoch with Tiger Woods. He is perhaps the most globally famous athlete since Muhammad Ali. Television ratings leap whenever he is in contention in a tournament. Prize money has reached levels only recently unimaginable. Professional golf as a spectator sport now sustains a superstructure comprising the main U.S. and European tours, various satellite tours for those who have not qualified for the main tours, special team and individual events, shorter winter tours in Africa and the Far East, numerous national and regional circuits, skin games, pro-ams, clinics, and exhibitions.

Yet golf seems unlikely as a spectator sport. Almost all sports, apart from certain types of motor racing and cross-country skiing and running events, are played in a single arena in which all the action is simultaneously visible. Golf, of course, is not. If you go to a golf course to watch a major event, you can follow a single group from start to finish, you can sit in a grandstand next to a green and watch the players putt as they pass through, you can run around trying to get glimpses of different players and different holes, or, perhaps most rewardingly of all, you can watch them hit balls on the practice ground. But you will never get the entire narrative of the day. If you try to see Tiger Woods, you will have to do so over or around a great many other heads. If you don't have a stool or a periscope, you may only see the sunlight flashing on the shaft of his club at the top of his backswing or follow-through. It is a highly fragmentary experience. On television you can at least get a sense of the entire picture of the event as it develops, but you will nevertheless spend most of your time watching the players trudge silently up the fairways or stalk the greens as they line up their putts or else following the progress of the white specks of their balls against the sky as the cameras waveringly track them. There is no sustained action in golf. It takes only around two seconds to hit a shot, then the player spends up to ten minutes or more walking after it and waiting to hit the next one.

Yet people watch in great numbers. Some of the greatest fortunes in all of sport have been amassed due to the yearning of people to watch professional golfers. Entire television channels are devoted to it. There is even one in Spain, where golf is of only marginal interest.

Can anything impede golf's march toward dominion? The professional game, the engine that drives everything else in the sport by disseminating its image and making people hungry to play it, could be threatened by two things, one scientific and the other economic. The equipment manufacturers' engineers strive daily to find ways of making golf balls go farther and straighter while staying within the club and ball specifications laid out in USGA and Royal and Ancient rules, while designers, greenkeepers, and tournament committees try to counteract this through lengthening, tightening, and the strategic placing of hazards and pins. A great course loses some of its dignity when its par fives are reachable with a drive and an eight iron. A par of seventy-two is thus reduced by four. Because the landmass of existing courses is already for the most part determined, the options open to those trying to defend them against the long ball are more limited than those open to the engineers. The economic threat could come from any serious downward movement in the economy. Professional golf depends on corporations putting up millions of dollars to sponsor tournaments as well as the purchase of advertising time on the networks that broadcast them. Tiger Woods alone can be enough to counteract the effect of most recessions, but if recession deepens into something worse, there will be fewer tournaments. There will also be less golf generally. The luxury developments with star designers, helicopter links from airports, on-course masseuses, and Augusta-level maintenance will face a declining market of super-rich lawyers and executives. This has already happened in Japan, where country clubs whose membership equities traded for up to $3.2 million each and where porters in tuxedos welcomed members at the clubhouse door are rapidly going bankrupt. Golf's plebeians will have less to spend on equipment and green fees, the retired may see their pensions crash along with the stock market, and municipalities struggling to maintain their schools and social services under increased demand may find their golf courses a low priority and close them. Still, the unemployed could in themselves be a significant market, for golf is a fine and distracting way to fill a long day. Perhaps, like the economically disadvantaged who were given apartments in luxurious developments in New York and London that went broke, unemployed golfers will find themselves on courses made for millionaires.

But let us assume that such an economic Armageddon will not take place. What, then, will be the effects of the great expansion of golf? Can golf transform character? Can it, when played by so many different people of so many different ages and types and races in so many different places, change in some way the global social fabric? Has there been a social effect in England from the playing in schools, military barracks, and village greens of cricket, that game so cunning and polite and vicious, or in America from the mass playing from so early an age of violent and fiercely competitive sports in which cheating is rewarded? I don't know. It would seem impossible to measure.

But if I were to speculate? There are, I would say, verifiably negative effects on the world from the playing of golf. Of all games it is probably the most domestically intrusive. It takes nearly all day to play and get back and forth from the course, and then golfers talk about it during so much of the time when they are not playing. And there is no clear prospect of the intrusion on family life having an endpoint, for unless gravely handicapped or ill the golfer can play the game until he dies. A *New Yorker* cartoon depicts a man with a golf bag on his shoulder looking back at his wife as he leaves the house, saying, "Gotta run, sweetheart. By the way, that was one fabulous job you did raising the children." The golfer's family may regard the game as an indulgence, and an extravagant, preposterous, and intolerable indulgence at that. But that is not how the golfer sees it. For him it is not a pastime. It is a *necessity*.

Golf can generate terrible moods. People so often begin a round in hope and end it in self-loathing. A friend of mine has described the sensations he has upon arrival at a golf course—a surging elevation of mood brought about by the smell of the grass, the vision of rolling fairways, and the hunger he inevitably feels in hands and mind and internal organs for striking golf balls. Seventeen and a half holes later he can be seen walking briskly in the rough beside the final fairway, head down, a scowl set on his face, as though someone has just vandalized his car. People who are normally equable and considerate can become surly, irritable, and self-pitying. They can lose their sense of proportion about the importance in the larger scheme of things of their weight shift or the position of their elbows at the midpoint of their backswing. Golf can perhaps even permanently cloud a sensibility, or so Scott Fitzgerald seems to have thought when he wrote in *The Great Gatsby,* "The bored haughty face that she turned to the world concealed something—most affectations concealed something eventually, even though they don't in the beginning—and one day I found out what it was. . . . At her first big golf tournament there was a row that nearly reached the newspapers—a suggestion that she had moved her ball from a bad lie in the semi-final round."

The particular kind of rage that golf generates is insidious and progressive. A player in a bad round can think he is being phlegmatic about his gruesome play, maintaining the bonhomie that the traditions of the game ask of him. He can think his dignity is intact.

But each skulled, shanked, and fat shot has taken its toll, for after a certain point a two-foot putt that does not even touch the hole can suddenly breach a frontier and a mild-mannered person can in an instant become a profane monomaniac. It is an ugly spectacle that anyone watching would find ludicrous, embarrassing, and ill-fitting an adult person.

There are unique complexities and contradictions in the rage that besets golfers. The vile shot is made, there is a sudden adrenaline-like surge within and then a need to lacerate oneself, embed a club in the skull, destroy the instrument that has so badly misstruck the ball. I have hit myself so hard on the forehead with the butt of my hand that my ears were left ringing for nearly half an hour. As this surge subsides and the player stalks off in search of his ball, the rage is replaced by an all-encompassing sense of worthlessness. He feels he does not deserve to be regarded as a golfer. But, strangely, the feeling is mixed with a sense of victimhood, as though an injustice has occurred. The rage turns in the direction of the universe generally. "How can this be happening to me?" the player seems to be pleading. Somewhere in the feeling too there is determination. The player will have his vengeance. The bad shot, he thinks, will be punished and consigned to oblivion by an extended display of magnificent ball-striking. This is of course unlikely, because the bad shot is so memorable, and the anger that ensued so damaging to the player's rhythm. Vanity is also present, for the player tries to distance himself from his poor shot by the ostentatiousness with which he expresses his rage, as if to imply that it was not his true golfing self that hit it.

None of these things can be good for a person's reputation, his soul, or his golf.

Golf has smaller worlds within itself based upon prejudice and social elitism. It can pollute with its pesticides and fertilizers. It can appropriate vast amounts of water and land from scarce resources. A Mallorcan friend of mine once said to me, "The descendants of our farmers and artisans have learned servility as waiters. Our un-harvested almond and olive trees have become tourist attractions. We have almost no water but we have more than twenty-five golf courses, even though Mallorcans don't play golf. Do you know any-one in Ireland who would know how to blow up golf courses?"

But golf is also healthy. It acquaints one with nature, or at least with some highly husbanded version of nature. It can be ecologi-cally beneficial. It promotes comradeship. It is inclusive. It is a game at which the weak can have an even chance to defeat the strong. This is because of handicapping. Handicapping is not a fa-vor bestowed patronizingly by the better player on the poorer one. It is scientifically arrived at and intrinsically part of the game.

Arnold Palmer thinks that golf can help to promote world peace. Who knows? I don't, certainly. But it can at least be said that it is a nonviolent sport in which civility and generosity are para-mount and dishonesty a disgrace. When Bobby Jones was congrat-ulated for calling a penalty on himself for his ball having moved in the rough after he addressed it, even though no one saw it happen and even though it could be said to have cost him victory in the U. S. Open, he replied, "You may as well congratulate a man for not robbing a bank."

Golf is, if not unique, then at least highly unusual among sports in its insistence on forms of behavior that are unusually complex in their delicacy and ornateness. There are ceremonies of greeting and leave-taking and the bestowing of praise, and rigorous standards regarding the order and pace of play. A solemn silence and stillness must reign when another is executing his shot, and neither shadows nor footprints in his putting line must in any way molest him. The tending of the course by the players is virtually commensurate with personal hygiene. There are no uniforms, but there are assumptions about what is acceptable to wear. The rule book is both inviolable and indisputable. Displays of petulance, self-congratulation, or tedious shot-by-shot narratives of one's round can befoul a reputation. Above all, to cheat is to place oneself utterly beyond the pale. So seriously was the charge of cheating taken by a member of an English club that when he was accused of it by another member, he sued for slander and fought the case in the courts and in the newspapers, nearly bankrupting himself.

All of these practices are ingested virtually with the air in the golf-playing nations, particularly Scotland, where the play is brisk, the competition robust, the appreciation of well-made shots deeply felt, and tolerance for deviation from the codes low. I once played at Gleneagles with a Glaswegian railwayman named Harry Campbell, who watched with a stern expression a slow-playing fourball of Americans ahead of us until finally calling out, "Would ye kindly expedite your game please!"—a courtly phrase delivered with incontrovertible ferocity. We were immediately let through.

But even in countries with a briefer acquaintance with golf, good etiquette on the course generally becomes second nature, so that when a player watches the flight of his opponent's ball, willing it all the while into a bunker, he is still able to exclaim "Fine shot!" with genuine feeling if it finishes dead to the pin. But the game's inner dynamics challenge one's ability to maintain this etiquette. Golf is so full of catastrophe and frustration that courtliness can seem a distant consideration. It is also intensely competitive. Severiano Ballesteros expressed this duality when answering a question about how he faced match play. "I go to the first tee, I shake my opponent's hand, clap him on the back, and wish him good luck," he said. "Then I think to myself, 'I will bury you.'" Some players cross the line, even the best. I have heard of three British Open champions who regularly lowered themselves to acts of gamesmanship that transgressed fundamental principles of the game. One made sure his feet were visible to his opponent as he addressed the ball and then wriggled his toes during the player's backswing. Another rattled coins in his pocket. The third regularly developed a timely cough in the midst of his opponent's putting stroke. I saw the last of these champions blatantly cheat during a British Open at Troon when with whispers and hand signals he asked the caddy of another player which club he had used on the par three seventeenth. I so long admired his play and so often willed for him to win that I cannot bring myself to write his name here. But, despite the provocations and temptations offered by golf, cheating is rare, whether at amateur or professional level. It is seen as a solitary and repellant vice. The golfing cheat will be known for this one trait above all others, as the man who never buys a round is known only as a scrounge by his drinking companions. The same, of course, cannot be said of any of the team games, where cheating is often admired.

The galumphing gaits of portly middle-aged hackers as they try not to step on one another's lines on the greens, their mumbled praise of "Well done!" or "Good weight!" or the cathedral-like silence in which they play may appear ridiculous to outsiders. But golf has held up well in large part through its adherence to standards of etiquette, which are based not so much in neurotic fastidiousness as in common sense, honesty, and respect. Golf demands respect and generates empathy. It insists that the land be left in as good a state as it was found. It is a game in which mind and body must work together in the most subtle of relationships, in which you are solely and manifestly accountable for what you have done, and in which you must strive to bear your hardships and your victories gracefully—though whether the spread of it can make for a worse or better world I cannot say.

4

·

Estrangement

I lived in exile from golf throughout most of the 1970s. I played
probably no more than a dozen times during my four years at university. Two weeks after finishing there I went to live on a deserted
island in Donegal, in the northwest of Ireland. There was a nine-
hole course in the dunes on the mainland, and I played a round
there among grazing sheep with a set of borrowed clubs that looked
as if they'd passed years leaning against the wall of a barn. I was in
the town one afternoon buying food and I saw a young woman with
long, thick, dark hair and a face for the ages sitting in a beam of
sunlight on the ledge of the post office window. I met her that night
in a pub with a racket of jigs and reels and Republican ballads
around us, and then she and the couple she was traveling with came

out to my little house on the island. Her name was Teresa. She left her shoes behind and I posted them to her.

I moved to Dublin when the cold autumn winds made life on the island no longer possible. I had the idea of going back to Donegal in the winter to try to get work on the herring boats, but before that I went over to London to visit Teresa. She worked in a bank there and lived in a compact little room in Shepherd's Bush that looked out onto an enormous tree in the back garden and had a cooker and a blow heater and lots of books and records but no refrigerator. I stayed with her there for four years before we moved north- and eastwards across the city. I never worked on the fishing boats nor lived in Ireland nor, apart from a few months, in the United States again. I got a job at a cash register assembly factory and then worked for a while for a left-inclining publisher. I was made redundant there in the midst of a struggle to get the union recognized. Teresa and I went to sessions where accordionists and fiddlers played and acted in plays at an Irish theater in the back of a pub in north London. I wrote overwrought stories that were full of posturing and inauthenticity. This went on for years. I wondered whether I would ever write a sentence in which I could believe. Eight years after I first saw Teresa on the post office window ledge in Donegal, we had a baby together, Aoife.

Many things interested me while I waited nervously for the words to take form and strike me. I knew I could wait indefinitely, but what if the words never arrived? I lived in the shadow of that. But I kept moving. I had the impression of living a crowded life into which golf did not fit. My parents brought my clubs over on one of their annual visits from Chicago, and I played some terrible rounds at public courses I could reach by bus or train. Golf still meant something to me. I remember the sudden feeling of elation I had when I read that Arnold Palmer had won tournaments in Canada and France late in his career. In theaters and cathedrals I would look up and wonder what club I would need to reach the upper gallery or the dome. But I no longer identified with golf in the way that I had. It had once been my principal form of self-expression and now no longer was, though its replacement was then only an aspiration at which I was even less developed than I had been at golf. I played sometimes but had ceased to think of myself as a golfer. I could not get a picture in my mind of the person I then thought I was and then transplant with ease and clarity that person onto a golf course.

At some point during this period my father met Chick Evans and Chick asked him how I was and if I was still playing golf. My father replied that I was fine but that I was playing very little as I was over in London without a car and without easy access to a course. I don't know in what way this information was conveyed, but Chick was sufficiently moved by it to try to intervene. He wrote an open letter to club secretaries of British golf clubs and had it delivered to my father, who then sent it on to me. The letterhead has a photograph of Chick in a golf hat surrounded by his trophies, and running down the left-hand margin is a list of some of his more important victories. The letter reads:

May 16, 1977

TO WHOMEVER IT MAY CONCERN:

I am taking the liberty, hoping my memories of seeing and playing many of the wonderful courses in Great Britain, of asking courtesies for the son of my outstanding Dentist whose name is Timothy E. O'Grady, 16 Bolingbroke Road, West Kensington, London W14, England.

The splendid father seems to think that his son has some depression due to his not being able to play his favorite game of golf.

I have enjoyed so many extremely fine friendships with British golfers and Clubs that I am emboldened to ask a great favor helping to arrange for him to have a course to play on every once in a while. I think Timothy has put an unreal value on all this.

Anything you can do for him will be a great kindness to me and a great compliment. I assure you that I will look for my time of reciprocity for trespassing on your valuable time.

I do hope Timothy can have some restrictions removed so that he can put his happiness trying to hit that uncertain ball.

Hopefully and gratefully yours,
Charles Evans Jr.

In its depiction of a morbidity induced by a drought of golf, I think the letter does not quite catch the person I then was, but it nevertheless startled and humbled me. Chick Evans reached the

ESTRANGEMENT

Charles Evans, Jr.
8 S. Michigan Ave.
Chicago, Illinois 60603
312/726-7741

Western Golf Association
Honorary Vice President

Evans Scholars Foundation
Honorary Trustee

—Major Titles—

U. S. Open (1916)

Western Open (1910)

U. S. Amateur (1916 & 1920)

Western Amateur (8 times)

University of Illinois
Man of the Year Award,
1976.

CHICK EVANS

May 16, 1977

TO WHOMEVER IT MAY CONCERN:

   I am taking the liberty, hoping my memories of seeing and playing many of the wonderful courses in Great Britain, of asking courtesies for the son of my outstanding Dentist whose name is Timothy E. O'Grady, 16 Bolingbroke Road, West Kensington, London W.14, England.

   The splendid father seems to think that his son has some depression due to his not being able to play his favorite game of golf.

   I have enjoyed so many extremely fine friendships with British golfers and Clubs that I am emboldened to ask a great favor helping arrange for him to have a course to play on every once in awhile. I think Timothy has put an unreal value on all this.

   Anything you can do for him will be a great kindness to me and a great compliment. I assure you that I will look for my time of reciprocity for trespassing on your valuable time.

   I do hope Timothy can have some restrictions removed so that he can put his happiness trying to hit that uncertain ball.

                    Hopefully and gratefully yours,

                    Charles Evans Jr

Secretary of Clubs around
London, England and those of the
British Isles.

highest point of American amateur golf by winning the U.S. Amateur twice, once in the same year that he won the U.S. Open. That was in 1916. No one had ever done that before, and the only person to do it afterward was Bobby Jones in 1930, the year of his Grand Slam. Harry Vardon, who had been defeated by the young American amateur Francis Ouimet in the 1913 U.S. Open, said that Chick was the best amateur he had played with in the United States. Jerry Travers, who had won the U.S. Amateur four times, said that "if Evans could putt like Walter J. Travis, it would be foolish to stage an amateur tourney in this country." It was like having W. H. Auden petition on your behalf for a pass to the British Library.

I hadn't a regular job for six years after I stopped working for the publisher. I worked for a while for the literary magazine *Transatlantic Review*. I copyedited manuscripts for London publishers. I moved furniture and worked in a box office. I wrote a history book called *Curious Journey: An Oral History of Ireland's Unfinished Revolution*. The book was published and I still feel well toward it, but I did not think it meant I had written a sentence in which I could believe, because none of the sentences was fiction. I sat in libraries and continued to write stories badly.

When the London Festival Ballet came to the Festival Hall for their summer and Christmas seasons in the late 1970s, I worked as a stagehand. I was a flyman on the off-prompt side. The entire crew was brought together only for those seasons, and when they weren't on, they did other things to make their livings. There was a short, round bearded impresario who imported Balinese dancers. There was a landscape gardener who had a doctorate in French colonial history. Two of the men in the wings worked on the shop floor of a furniture factory in the Caledonian Road in north London. A propsman was having an affair with a ballerina, and I think I had an oblique offer from one of them myself once, but I didn't take it up. Most of the dancers looked at us as if we were pieces of scenery.

On my fly floor there were two others apart from myself—an aesthete who'd read English at Oxford and subsequently sold wine, and a tall, bearded former student of astrophysics at Cambridge named Brian, who'd lived for a while in Hong Kong and seemed to have acquired a curiously Chinese look. He did *Times* crosswords on gantries high above the stage and invented complex machines with cranks and pulleys for flying the dancers off. He was also a golfer.

Through Brian I began to reenter the game. Sometimes after working through the night to get a show set up, a group of us would go for a pint in a Smithfield Market early-morning pub and then head to Richmond Park for a round of golf. I played appallingly. I'd swing so hard I'd nearly leave my feet and then top the ball to the front of the tee. We continued these games sporadically and there was a small improvement. I think I had a couple of reasonable scores at a nine-hole course in Dorking, where I remember eagling a par four after driving the green, perhaps twice. A first violin and another musician in the ballet's orchestra challenged Brian and me to a round at Royal Mid-Surrey, an old club that at one point draws near to the pagoda in Kew Gardens and on that day seemed to be full of retired senior civil servants and air marshals. I wore combat boots and torn jeans. Ridiculous, even if it were all I had available. Still, neither our hosts nor the venerable men in wicker chairs on the veranda commented.

I hit a few good shots. I remember a four wood to the green that I could not have wished to improve upon. But mostly it was wretched. Nevertheless, Brian pulled us through and we won the match.

These games with the stagehands left me with a mournful yearning for golf. I began taking an overground train from Hackney Downs out to a course in Chingford. I met a man named John Collins there, a housing project janitor who'd grown up in Mile End in the East End of London when it was dominated by the notorious gang led by the Kray twins. He and I and some of his friends played another round or two at Chingford and then moved across to the thirty-six-hole layout at Hainault, where we played early Sunday-morning rounds on the lower course with the odd outing during the week. I liked this course better than any other I'd yet played around London. It was wooded and hilly. It had only one par five, but there were some excellent par fours, particularly six and twelve. I'd get picked up at dawn, we'd play for a few pounds, and then we'd have fried eggs in the café after.

These men were older than me and relatively new to the game, but a couple of them played hard, particularly a half-Zulu, half-Irish park attendant named Vince. There was a lothario named John who drove a minicab by day and did Frank Sinatra impersonations in East End pubs at night and once brought one of his girlfriends out onto the course with him. We'd been hearing about her activities for weeks, and now there she was, twenty years younger than him, following him with wounded devotion while he concentrated on his game. There was an ex-boxer who'd had something of a career as a welterweight, but had the misfortune to coincide with the era of an overwhelmingly dominant fighter named John Stracey, who blocked the path to the British title of my golfing friend and every other fighter in the division. The club looked like a little twig in his hands. He could very occasionally hit the ball enormous distances, but he liked to call me The Gorilla whenever I caught a drive well. Taxi drivers played there, as did stallholders from the Ridley Road market in Dalston. You'd see Ford shiftworkers from the Dagenham plant with poor swings who played off five because their timing was so good after years of daily golf. The people I played with were thrilled to have discovered golf. They thought it should be kept a secret because if everyone knew how wonderful it was, all the courses would be overwhelmed.

I finally found a sentence and wrote it down and then kept writing for four and a half years until I had a novel, which I called *Motherland.* I retreated again from golf during that time. I had a couple of jobs, there was the book, and then in the last months of writing it I had the operation on my back. I sat up in my bed on the ward when the others were asleep and kept on writing. I played my first round of golf after recuperating at Ruislip, west London, with the writer Caryl Phillips. On the first hole I hit a drive down the right side, knocked a short iron up onto the green about forty feet past the hole, then rolled in the putt for a birdie. Until that hole I had not struck a single shot in eighteen months. This is the kind of thing golf feeds you before kneeing you in the groin.

In the absence of playing I talked about golf, if I found someone sufficiently sympathetic. But I was becoming aware that this was not so easy. I often had the idea that many people I met around London felt that golf was something about which one should be embarrassed, like having brass rubbing as a hobby, or being a Freemason, that it was solely for the rich, the pampered, the vulgarly aspirant. This surprised me. Golf was a game. You could be mesmerized by it, as I was, or indifferent toward it, but I didn't understand why anyone would allocate a portion of their energy to despising it. Animals weren't killed in it, or at least that was not its purpose. People were not maimed.

At some point during this time I met the poet Matthew Sweeney. We were at a party in London given by the Irish man of letters Anthony Cronin, also a poet as well as the biographer of Samuel Beckett. Most of the people there were in some way connected with the world of books, reviewing or publishing or writing them. Golf would have been as alien a topic there as needlework or sheep dipping. Yet Matthew and I managed to discover that we were both golfers. It was almost as if we'd been told that we were cousins. I remember him turning with a slack jaw and saying slowly to his wife, *"He plays golf,"* with both awe and relief. He not only played, but had also written poems on the subject, among them a description of a former gambling partner of his named Big Frank, who was considerably senior to him. The poem reads:

BIG FRANK

Often in the dregs of daylight
he'd be on the course,
or if not, he'd want me to be—

his travelling partner,
his teenage accomplice, or worse.
Lights on, he'd come to check me.
Knowing my silhouette,
he'd leave the engine running,
and, chuckling accompaniment,
"Nocturnal walloper," he'd shout.
Weekends, we'd do the rounds
of the county's courses—
we'd lurk in the car
till he saw a likely pair
approach the clubhouse.
Straight away he'd challenge them
for a fiver a head.
"Me and the boy," he'd say
in his suspect way.
"We'll take you on. How's that?"
Out on the tee, he'd whisper:
"Drop your club when they hit.
Cough when they putt.
They won't expect any better.
They know you're a kid."
But I was too arrogant
for that. I *knew* we would win.
I could swing the club
(in this I was wrong)
and I wasn't playing alone.

And he had all the style—
birdies from well off the green.
Lying on his mouth and nose
to line up the putt,
then rattling it in
under the turned-up toe
and the grimace; the grunt
to match my cheer
as I ran to claim the ball,
savouring the affront
to likeliness. He had his éclats
in his singular way,
and I was his sidekick,
his fifteen-year-old straight man,
and no one could say
we didn't try to lick them,
didn't very often win
on the 18th green—
or in open competition
as the last pair in.

We began to play, him in a cloud of mournfulness and me on
and sometimes over the edge of apoplexy. With him there came his
hypochondria, more refined and imaginative than any I had ever
known. One day we were sitting together in the back of a friend's
car on our way to a golf course, with him describing knee pains and

professional slights, when he saw a garbage truck ahead. "Keep your distance from that truck," he counseled the driver. "There's a certain kind of flying insect, a red one, always around trucks like that. If they get into your ear they can *melt your brain.*"

For years he'd suffered attacks at parties, such as the one we met at, for being a golfer. People would openly yawn in his face at the mention of the word *golf.* He now regarded me as an ally, as though we were in the same cult and needing to fortify our defenses together against an ignorant world. If he saw an attack coming, he would summon me urgently and we would launch a double-barreled riposte. In time defense turned to offense and we began to goad people into disparaging golf so that we could let them have the full force of our now well-developed speech on the superiority of our favorite game.

Golf seemed to so many people to be in poor taste. The most common charge was that it was a game only for snobs. Perhaps the charge of snobbery is more readily to hand in a country like England with its acute sensitivity to gradations of class. My own experience of golf had been entirely the reverse of what appeared to be a general impression of golf courses as being the most obvious and repellent of the many playgrounds of the bourgeoisie. All my golfing life I had been playing with people of different ages, races, and levels of income on cheap, municipal courses. I thought that golf, which allowed for competition as equals by players of all abilities, was the most democratic and open of sports. It is also, with tennis, the most international of ball games. I had met a far wider variety of people through golf than I had through, for example, university or drinking in pubs. It is unlikely that I would have known the men I played with at Hainault had it not been for golf. Golf creates friendships that would otherwise be unlikely to exist. It was not that I was unaware that there were snobs who played golf. I had worked at a private club. I knew that many private clubs, perhaps most, were closed off from the world, were full of infantile prejudices and were designed to make their members feel that they ruled their countries, or at least their little patches of them. But would anyone judge university education by an Oxford high table, or public houses by the bar at Claridge's? Golf is as much for the Glasgow postman on the bus with his clubs as it is for the corporate executive.

And the clubs are not always as they may superficially seem, particularly the older and more traditional of the British ones. They are made for an elite but they nevertheless abhor ostentation. The members sit around in the bar in their dun-colored golf attire like schoolboys in uniform, privileged collectively but equal among themselves. Displays of wealth or personal importance have a rank odor in this milieu. They can result in ostracization. This ethos is embodied in the club secretary, an employee but also a disciplinarian and custodian of the codes. My accountant told me that one day at Ganton in Yorkshire, one of the finest of Britain's inland courses, a white Rolls-Royce advanced up the driveway in front of the clubhouse and parked next to a sign that said No Parking. Two men wearing suits got out of the car. They were smoking cigars. They walked across the lawn past a sign that read, "Please do not walk on the grass." The club secretary was standing on the clubhouse steps with a clipboard with the day's starting times in his hand, looking at them out of narrowed eyes. The men stopped in front of him.

"Are you the caddy master?" they asked.

"That's right, men," said the club secretary, "and we have no need of caddies today."

I also encountered around London the idea that golf could hardly be thought of as a sport, that it was something between lawn bowling and rambling, but less demanding and more artificial than either. A person who has not played golf could not reasonably be expected to know of the enormous labor that goes into playing it well, of the infinitesimally precise degree of coordination and control required, or of the mental and physical endurance required by tournament play. But then nor should such people expect, in their ignorance, to be free to pass judgment on it. Several of the people I met making these and other charges were book reviewers, journalists, and other media and public relations people, or actresses just back from a yoga class. Many fit the privileged, elitist, socially and materially aspirant prototypes that they attacked golf for harboring, though they went about their aspiring in a different style. Behind this charge that golf was not a sport was the idea that it was a game for sissies, or for those too old or unfit to do anything else. So confident were they in making this charge that one would think they passed their spare time bullfighting or sparring with Oscar de la Hoya. William Hazlitt was repeatedly abused for his enthusiasm for boxing, which he called the Fancy, and, articulate as he was about so many things, had this to say in reply: "Ye who despise the Fancy, do something to show as much pluck, or as much self-possession as this, before you assume a superiority which you have never given a single proof of by any one action in the whole of your lives." I only came upon this recently. I wish I had known it earlier.

What they are saying is that golf is uncool. They don't like the clothes. They don't like the physiques. It is played by the old, the fat, the suburban, the unglamorous. It is played by provincial Rotarians wishing to increase their business contacts and confirm their social status.

But golf is wider than that. Machinists, security guards, short-order cooks, and hookers are golfers. Ghetto residents and jazz singers. Michael Jordan, the notoriously self-destructive Irish snooker player Hurricane Higgins, and Ivan Lendl play golf. Oscar de la Hoya as well, as it happens. Joe Louis played and ran his own tournament in Detroit for black professionals. Samuel Beckett played a kind of minimalist golf using only four clubs yet attained a handicap of seven. He was an insomniac and, when asked what he did to try to get to sleep, replied, "I play in my mind the first nine holes of the Carrickmines Golf Club near Dublin, and if that doesn't work, I play the back nine as well." Robert Graves played with Siegfried Sassoon. The Irish novelist Aidan Higgins set a course record in Wicklow. Rudyard Kipling learned golf from Arthur Conan Doyle and painted his golf balls red so he could play in the snow when he was living in New England. Anthony Trollope used to bellow his way around the course. He once collapsed onto the green in grief over a missed putt, but then immediately sprang up again yelping in pain as he had landed on a golf ball in his pocket. Meat Loaf,

Madonna, and Sharon Stone all play. Jack Nicholson is a single-handicap player. Alice Cooper has played off four and advertises Callaway golf clubs on television. Willie Nelson owns a course called Pedernales. Dennis Hopper played with him there when he was making *The Texas Chainsaw Massacre II* and said about it, "The dress code there was like men could basically wear anything, but they'd prefer them to keep their pants on. Women, they didn't care, but they'd prefer them not to keep their pants on." Hopper started to play golf to have something to do after he forswore drugs and alcohol, but had difficulty finding a club that would accept him, as, he said, had Victor Mature many years before when he applied to the Los Angeles Country Club. "We're sorry, Mr. Mature," they said, "but we don't accept actors here." "Actors?" said Mature. "Nobody's ever accused me of being an actor before." Hopper was finally accepted at Riviera in Pacific Palisades, but continued from time to time to play in a threeball with Neil Young and Bob Dylan at a Japanese-owned public course near Malibu. Young, whose brother is a professional, is a good player and once competed in a tournament organized by Eddie Van Halen. Dylan too evidently plays a respectable game. "He's sort of taken it up," says Hopper. Iggy Pop plays well enough, evidently, to have given lessons to Lou Reed. Alice Cooper said of him, "I used to call Iggy about where to score drugs. Now when I call we talk about our backswings." Joe Pesci and Samuel L. Jackson play, as do numerous cricket, basketball, ice hockey, baseball, and football players. Che Guevara played as a young man in Argentina and again later in combat fatigues on a course in Cuba after the revolution. Probably not many book reviewers play. They may fear the exposure.

Some of those who play have also written about it. In 1743 Thomas Mathison wrote a long poem in cantos called "The Goff: An Heroi-Comical Poem," in which Castalio vanquishes Pygmalion on the final green by knocking in a shot "full fifteen clubs' lengths from the hole." Tobias Smollet watched a group of golfers on the links at Leith, the youngest of whom was eighty, and who, he said, "had amused themselves with this pastime for the best part of a century, without ever having felt the least alarm from sickness or disgust; and they never went to bed without having each the best part of a gallon of claret in his belly." Arthur Balfour, the British prime minister, wrote perceptively about golf. The English poet laureate John Betjeman wrote a poem about birdieing the thirteenth hole at Saint Enodoc, which includes the lines "A glorious, sailing, bounding drive / That made me glad I was alive." William Faulkner played and began *The Sound and the Fury* with the sentence "Through the fence, between the curling flower spaces, I could see them hitting." Ford Madox Ford, Ian Fleming. A. A. Milne, Julian Barnes, George MacDonald Fraser, Walker Percy, Richard Ford, and Damon Runyon have all written about golf. John Updike has written enough articles, stories, and parts of novels about golf to form a collection, which he called *Golf Dreams.* He is particularly eloquent about bad shots. But P. G. Wodehouse must be judged supreme among writers of golf fiction. His collection of stories about the Oldest Living Member runs to nearly five hundred pages. "There are three things in the world that he held in the smallest

esteem—" wrote Wodehouse in his story "Rodney Fails to Qualify," "slugs, poets and caddies with hiccoughs."

"Golf converts oddly well into words," wrote Updike. All sports
express powerful forces in life—despair and triumph, courage and
endurance, the stretching of nerve and physical strength to their
limits—and as such have provided a focus for literature. That they
are generally acted out according to precise rules in confined spaces
and under the scrutiny of spectators tends to isolate and intensify
these emotions, throwing them into relief more in the manner of art
than of life. But some sports have proven more alluring than others.
Boxing, for example, has compelled more writers and drawn more
out of them than lacrosse. The same could be said of cricket,
rugby, and baseball, as opposed to ice hockey or hammer throwing.

Golf, a minority sport, has attracted a disproportionate quantity
of words. This can be seen by looking at the sports section of any
bookstore. Why is that? Golf 's great age, perhaps, or the opportu-
nities it provides for observing relations among the different classes
or the sexes. Metaphors abound in golf writing—for the different
shots, wonderful or outrageous, and the players' reactions to them.
Allegory is well suited to golf because a round is a journey full of
obstacles and temptations. It is also inherently comic, because it
is played with such intense seriousness and hopefulness and the
results are so often appalling.

But perhaps the real reason why so many writers have been
drawn to golf is that it is so much like writing itself. It is solitary in
its execution. It is complex and unconquerable and demands a long
apprenticeship. It is pitilessly exposing. You cannot fake anything

and there is nowhere to hide and no one to blame. Purity is rarely attained in either activity, yet the desire for it in each escalates into obsession.

I got my first opportunity to write about golf in 1991 when a friend of mine working for *Esquire* magazine in London phoned me to say that they were preparing a supplement about golf and asked if I would like to contribute to it. For my first assignment I went north to the Dunlop-Slazenger club- and ball-manufacturing works in Normanton, West Yorkshire, to watch a robot called Metal Max test clubs and balls on their driving range. Metal Max could hit drives farther than John Daly if programmed to do so. The day I was there he was hitting low, Lee Trevino–like fades. Writing about golf was eventually to get me to wonderful and expensive courses I would certainly never otherwise have played and brought me into contact with people I would never otherwise have met. I had a conversation with Jose Maria Olazabal for an hour in his hotel room in Málaga. Afterward he let me swing his three iron out on the lawn. I said I had hoped we could play a round together, but as this had not been possible perhaps we could imagine it. "Fine," he said. "How are we doing?" "I'm three up after fourteen," I said. He feigned shock. "I must go to the practice tee," he said. I had another hour with Tom Watson on the lawn in front of the clubhouse at Royal Saint George's at the British Open in the year that he captained the American Ryder Cup team. He made a number of trenchant and interesting observations, but the one I remember above all was his description of his worst memory as a professional. He was at a tournament and was walking in the parking lot carrying his golf bag and a little case with some clothes and shoes after a round that had displeased him. As he approached his car, a boy walked up to him holding a program. "He said to me, 'Would you sign this please, Mr. Watson?' I said, 'Can't you see I've got my hands full?' I was tired and disappointed in the way I'd played, but that was no excuse. His face just fell and he turned away. His father walked up then and said, 'Mr. Watson, I'd just like to let you know what a jerk I think you are.' He was right of course. I felt absolutely terrible, and I've never forgotten it."

And I visited Watson's mentor, Byron Nelson, on the farm on the outskirts of Fort Worth he bought after retiring from the tour in his thirties, having won all the majors save the British Open and, in 1945, eleven tournaments in a row. I had long thought of him as perhaps the kindest and most empathetic of the players of his era, but he was also, at ninety-two, still formidable in speech and imposing physically. We sat in his study under a photograph of him and Watson, for whom he once hand made a wooden chest. We hadn't as much time as I would have liked as he was due to accompany his wife to church, but I was able to ask him about his greatest strength as a player. "Snead always said I was the best driver of the ball," he said. "I don't know if that was necessarily true. But I do know that compared with others I was able to play easy golf. Some of them were going along at ninety miles per hour, but I coasted along at sixty. Sometimes I pushed it up to seventy, but I always tried to keep it easy. I didn't know I had that record streak of wins going until a reporter asked me about it. When Vijay had ten or twelve top tens in a row, the PGA called me to ask how many I'd had. I hadn't any idea. So they did some research and phoned back to tell me."

"How many was it?" I asked.

"Sixty-seven," he replied.

Such encounters of course made me feel privileged, but the most pleasing thing of all about writing about golf was the unexpected sensation of this game so thwarting in the playing seeming to convert "oddly well into words." I was pleased, and grateful, finally to be writing fiction after fearing for more than ten years that I might never do it. But it was incomparably the hardest thing I had ever attempted. A normal day involved three hours of walking around a small room and staring at its walls, followed by a staggering run of a few hundred words, several or all of which might be excised the next or some other day. An inchoate idea exists somewhere in your consciousness that has a sufficient urgency to make you want to express it, and then in another place is such knowledge and sense of form and capacity to name as you might possess. You try to bring them all into alignment. You do this with each sentence and each sentence is done blind. It is an act of controlled abandon, like a golf swing, except that unlike a golf swing each sentence is unrepeatable. You are forever entering this idea, or attempting to enter it, and then leaving it, and at any point you could enter by the wrong door. You might never enter by the right door. You are never free of anxiety. You live with the fear of insufficiently serving the idea that has somehow been given you. Such, at least, has been my experience. But writing about golf, I found, was utterly different. I had a good time doing it. It felt simple, fluid, natural. I'd felt many things writing fiction, including, rarely, excitement. But I'd never felt easeful pleasure. Writing about golf had that—an easeful pleasure. I'd get to the end of a day and be disinclined to stop. I had the feeling I could go on doing it around the clock. It never involved those grinding, mind-splitting efforts at concentration that make you eager to flee the task. It just seemed to roll out. There was a feeling in this of liberation.

5

·

Professionals

My father told me that any illusions he might momentarily have harbored about there being only a narrow margin of difference between a good amateur and a professional were broken forever by a
single shot struck during a round he played in California. The shot
was made by a touring professional who had once won the PGA
Championship. I don't remember his name or the reason my father
was playing with him. The pro had had an injury and was just then
beginning to gently play his way back into the game after recuperating. His play was a little erratic. There was not much of a difference
between his score and my father's. On one hole the pro hit a drive
way out to the right onto an adjacent fairway. He was around two
hundred yards from the green with a line of high trees blocking his

route all the way. He took out a mid-iron and hit it straight down the line of the fairway he had landed on, parallel to the one on which he was meant to be playing. My father did not understand the idea of this shot until somewhere near the apex of the ball's trajectory, when it suddenly turned directly left in the air like one of those toy cars directed by remote-control panels, swinging some forty yards over the trees at a sharp angle to its original line of flight before dropping gently onto the green. My father had never seen a shot like that before. He could hit fades and draws in varying parabolic arcs, but he had never imagined a ball could be made to behave in the way he had just seen. He knew that no matter how many times the shot's execution was explained to him and how much effort he devoted to practicing it, he would never be able to hit it. He had good hands, but his hands could not be made to do that.

I had a similar experience when playing with a club pro named Doug Wood at the Jasper Park course in the Canadian Rockies. I was traveling in a large group, and when the others were hungover, Doug and I went out early in the morning and played at a blinding lick, the whole of the eighteen holes in two hours and something. "This is what it's all about," he said as we galloped between shots. He was spending most of his time selling sweaters in his shop at Banff and his game was a little ragged. He was beating me, but not by a lot. There is a wonderful par four at Jasper Park, the fourteenth, set down beside a lake, the hole doglegging left along the shoreline. Elk were strolling around behind the tee when we got there. We both hit our second shots right of the green, behind a line of low shrubs, too close to try to pop the ball over. "We're stymied,

Doug," I said to him. "There's no such thing as a stymie," he said, and took out a wedge, hooded it a little, and rolled his wrists over at impact. It was a little chip-and-run shot and he *hooked* it, the ball actually bending left slightly around the shrub even though it was airborne for no more than forty feet. It took a hard left kick when it hit the edge of the green because of all the spin he'd put on it, then ran down to about four feet from the hole, on the low side. I'd stood behind him to watch the shot, and when he'd done it, I wondered whether it was somehow an optical illusion, something to do with the water and the lie of the land. I wondered too whether he'd got the left kick because the ball hit a bump on the fringe of the green. But when I looked at all the different angles, I found that the shot must have worked as I had originally perceived it. It was all spin. If someone had told me about this shot, I'd have had great difficulty believing it.

A good pro will beat an amateur in almost every instance. Pros make a higher percentage of solid strikes, they have more shots available to them with each club, their misses are less catastrophic, they're better around the greens, and they think better. They have a good idea of the percentage of risk with each shot, and they know what to do with this knowledge. They have both an empirical and an intuitive sense of when to lay back and when to turn on the power and play most of the time well within their capacities. They tend not to unravel after an atrocious shot or hole. Each knows with scientific exactitude his own game in all its many varieties and has several ways of salvaging a poor situation and exploiting a good one. An English pro told me that he's placed respectably in tournaments in which he was badly out of rhythm by hitting each full shot half-strength. "It was embarrassing," he said. "But I was able to make good scores." The entire demeanor of professionals from the time they get out of their cars to the moment they put their clubs away is different from the amateur's. You can see their skill, their confidence, their intimacy with the game, in the methodical way they go about their work, their familiarity with their instruments, the way their gestures and their gaits and their swings are all of a piece rhythmically. There is a silence about them, a slowness, an authoritative calmness. They appear self-sufficient.

Perhaps all athletes have this. I saw the same look on the faces of a line of bullfighters in the lobby of a hotel in Bilbao. They were still, passive, calm, and imposing. Perhaps the ability to express oneself at the highest level physically obviates the fretful urgency to express oneself through spoken words. Musicians have this too, I have noticed, once they reach a certain level. Words can be serviceable, pleasant, or entertaining, but they are not the principal form of expression for them. They have become redundant.

But what distinguishes a great professional, a multiple winner of major championships, from a good one? What constitutes the journey he makes? I can only guess. Many are gifted athletically and excelled at other sports. This would suggest an innate agility, strength, good hand-eye coordination, and competitiveness. Perhaps too an instinctive grasp of the body's dynamics. Jack Nicklaus was an excellent basketball player. Babe Zaharias was an Olympic champion in track and field, and Patty Berg was a speed skater. Sam Snead, Walter Hagen, and Raymond Floyd seriously considered professional baseball careers. Paul McGinley, who may never win a major championship but who will forever be remembered for his putt on the eighteenth at the Belfry to win the 2002 Ryder Cup for Europe, was a fine Gaelic football player. Some have unusual physical attributes. John Daly can rotate his shoulders 12 percent farther than is normal on the tour, allowing him to get himself into a position where his club is pointing down at the ground at the top of his backswing. And there must be something equally peculiar in Sergio Garcia's wrists, as there was in Ben Hogan's, that he hits the ball so late. Sam Snead, even in advanced years, could kick the ceiling of a bar from a standing position for a bet. He had the most admired swing in all of golf—"the most fluid, natural, and authentic," as Arnold Palmer described it. Snead was said to be "double-jointed," but he said his joints were just unusually loose.

Almost all the great players entered the game when very young, practiced to the point of exhaustion, and quickly became prodigious—eerily so in the case of Tiger Woods. There is a story told to a journalist by Tiger's father about him proposing to a local pro that he play a match with his gifted son. If Tiger won, he was to be granted playing privileges at the pro's course. The only stipulations were that Tiger play from the ladies' tees and be given a shot per hole. The pro agreed, they went out on the course, and Tiger won the match. "His age?" asked the journalist of Earl Woods. "Four," he replied.

Earl Woods was obsessed by golf, but was not a professional. Many fine players have fathers who were pros—David Duval, Davis Love III, Sergio Garcia, Arnold Palmer. Palmer said that his father set him up with the basic grip, stance, and swing plane and told him, "Now hit it hard, go find it, and hit it hard again." "I never managed to hit it quite hard enough to please him," said Palmer.

Great talent, I think, generates the will to bring that talent to fruition. As talent develops so does will, and as will develops so does talent. The two come to feed off each other. If a person has a singing voice sent down from the heavens, that person is likely to have a fascination with that voice, will look for all number of ways to give it depth, nuance, and authenticity, and finally will go any-where and do anything, including in some cases walking over the backs of those who are in the way, in order for that voice to be heard. It is only a stillborn thing unless it is sent out into the world. Some have the impression that geniuses are delicate and unworldly beings, and yet such is the power and originality of their products that the world doesn't know how to receive them and that therefore many masterpieces lie unknown in drawers or in attics. I think this is unlikely. Genius tends to demand to be heard. It creates its own hard skin, and capacity for endurance. James Joyce promulgated a myth about the lofty, detached artist, but when his first book was rejected more than forty times, he kept on until it found a home. Such was his self-belief and lack of detachment with respect to the grimy world of commerce, at least for as long as it needed to be en-gaged with to get his books published. This might also be called ambition, thought by many to be an ugly thing. But among the greatest of artists, as among the greatest of golfers, it is not gener-ally an ambition for money or fame or to grind others underfoot—though it may be an ambition for immortality. It is more to do with completing the act that began with the self-discovery of the talent, in the case of the golfer, or of the need, in the case of the artist, of expressing oneself and having that expression received by the world. "A skill unexpressed is an anguish," I read somewhere— skill as an athlete, a doctor, an artist, a lover. But a skill expressed is an exuberance. When I interviewed Tom Watson, he said, "Golf for me was a means of expressing myself. I was silent much of the time when I was young. Even the idea of speaking to people I didn't know was something I found paralyzing. But golf was something through which I discovered I could express myself and establish my presence, be somehow acknowledged in the world."

Self-expression is onanistic without someone receiving it. You can sense this in the face of a child struggling with words, the fervid need to reach another person and be understood. The drive to do this, I believe, is as profound and elemental as the will to survive. It is the depth and intensity of this drive that makes the difference between the good and the great. Arnold Palmer was asked what he thought his greatest strength as a player had been. Year after year golf magazines judged him the best long iron player in the game. He was renowned for his power, his attacking play, his ability to escape from trouble, and his fearless putting. But his answer included none of these things. "Desire," he said.

Talent and desire are often first made visible through the devotion to practice. Sylvia Plath wrote one thousand villanelles during one of her summer holidays from university. Jimi Hendrix was known to have wandered around for days with his guitar, ceaselessly plucking it. Golf professionals practice in a way that seems to reach the borderlands of mania and for amounts of hours unequaled in other sports. When Walter Hagen was a boy, he built his own four-hole course in a cow pasture and was in it the whole of the day. When he was a university student, Jack Nicklaus could be seen hitting balls long into the night into a field, lit by the headlights of his father's car. Ben Hogan hit six hundred balls every day before lunch, then played eighteen holes in the afternoon. He believed that if he took two or three days off from this regime, he would feel the negative effects for up to three months. Vijay Singh is said to practice eight hours per day. During tournaments he can be seen carrying his clubs into his hotel so that he can continue practicing in his room. A Spanish friend of mine who knew him when he was just starting on the European tour was alarmed at the sight of him banging balls all day and finally into the darkening sky. "Vijay, you're a professional, you have to practice, but please, enough is enough!" "If you saw where I came from," said Vijay, "you'd practice like this too." After his outstanding 2004 season he was asked if he ever went on vacation. "I wouldn't know what to do," he said.

No player has, to my knowledge, reached the heights of the game without at some early point in his life hitting balls all day and every day for a considerable period. Severiano Ballesteros is thought to have excelled through inspiration, feel, and a celestially bestowed swing. He went out onto the beach at Pedrena with his three iron as a child, and his golf was thereafter sustained by the pure magic of his being. Such is the myth. I saw him practice at Málaga. He arrived from Dubái having just won a tournament. He warmed up on the practice ground for forty-five minutes, then played eighteen holes with four balls on every hole. He gave a press conference, had lunch, and then went back to the practice ground for three hours to hit high, drawn four irons, a shot he was working on for Augusta. He pitched and chipped for half an hour, then joined the other pros on the putting green. One by one they left. Finally even his caddy left. It was dark. He stayed alone for nearly another hour practicing his putting in the spill of the dining room lights through the clubhouse window.

Practicing in this way can seem from the outside to be tedious, grueling, even physically painful. But I think the professionals themselves, at least the best of them, find it fascinating. Ben Hogan's practice habits were thought by some to be a kind of self-flagellation. But he loved it. "I couldn't wait to get up in the morning and hit golf balls," he said. Everyone's game is in flux and every swing is both unique and susceptible to multitudinous influences, but only good players are acutely sensitive to this and know how to correct and evolve and understand how their mind and body are in each circumstance. They practice to correct flaws, to inculcate technical changes, to tune their timing and tempo, to instill a workable swing deeply in the memory of the muscles so that it will repeat even under the most trying of circumstances, but also, I think, to get close to the unreachable heart of the game. "I am waiting for the day when everything falls into place," said Tom Watson, "when everything makes sense, when every swing is with confidence and every shot is exactly what I want. I know it can be done. I've been close enough to smell it a couple of times, but I'd like to touch it, to feel it. I know it's been touched. Hogan touched it. Byron Nelson touched it. Then I think I could be satisfied. Then I think I could walk away from the game." But really there is no point at which the process ends. This is one of the great strengths of golf. I once met a woman in Soho in London, then a painter and still beautiful in her forties, who twenty years earlier had worked in an escort bar and earned more than any of the other girls because she wouldn't sleep with the customers. Golf ultimately derives its power and mystique from this same force—it is both everlastingly inviting and everlastingly inviolable.

Idolatry has set many on their way to greatness. Harold Pinter revered Beckett as Bob Dylan revered Woody Guthrie. Bobby Jones motivated the young Jack Nicklaus as subsequently Nicklaus motivated the young Nick Faldo. The spectacle of greatness is thrilling, alluring, intoxicating. It can make the beholder want to do the same thing, breathe the same air. In the case of the young golfer, if the interest has been ignited and the skill developed and displayed and the decision finally made to become a touring professional, what stands between him and the achievements of his hero? There are the other players, of course, around 150 of the world's best at every major championship. Even at a minor event on a satellite tour the practice ground is full of players with swings of repetitive, metronomic simplicity hitting shot after shot of apparent perfection. There are the technical flaws in one's game—something unreliable in the swing, erratic putting, wild driving. Even Jack Nicklaus was said to be weak with the wedge, generally thought by experts to be one of the three most important clubs in the bag, along with the driver and the putter.

But what will primarily impede a promising young player is the mind's resistance to assuming the forms and manners needed for the winning of a championship. A player must learn to contend with the loneliness and anonymity of life lived perpetually on the road, a problem compounded greatly for players with small children at home or with glamorous wives with time on their hands. He must learn to silence his mind, cauterize his emotions, and make his body robotic, unnatural though such things are. He is both a player and a businessman, and he must find a way of relating to the making of money that does not interfere with his playing. Money can be scarce for a player struggling to qualify for the tour, but not so many years ago it was scarce for nearly all touring professionals, particularly in Europe. Now there is so much money in professional golf through sponsorship and prize money even for players halfway down the money list that money in itself no longer provides the kind of win-or-starve motivation that drove Snead, Hogan, and Lee Trevino. Leading players are pampered wherever they go. They are surrounded by people whose incomes depend on serving and flattering them. The mind gets softened by luxury, the senses dulled by corporate drinks parties where the players must talk with people they are likely to feel no affinity toward. They can begin to feel that they are forever being bought, that they have gone from being a competitive athlete to the hired entertainment, like a strip-o-gram girl. Cynicism can become readily available. To be great they must maintain the simple, vigorous, and impassioned relationship with the game they began with. They must in the most fundamental way stay humble before it, as a musician must be humble toward his music or a writer toward language, for the game is of course more powerful than they are, and if they approach it with smugness, they will play it poorly. Yet this is not easy. Money and flattery, the endless selling of oneself and answering of the same tedious questions can sour a player's taste for the game. It can make it seem burdensome and artificial.

The young pro must also find a way of contending with anger, because he will almost certainly feel it. Golf is an enraging game. Bobby Jones said that when he played in his first U.S. Amateur, he and his opponent threw clubs so often that from behind they looked like a juggling act. Arnold Palmer threw a club over a tree in a school championship and was told by his father that if he did it again, he would not be allowed to play. Both Jones and Palmer found ways of not making spectacles of themselves, but certain others didn't. Tommy Bolt advised throwing one's club in the direction of the shot so that you could pick it up on the way. Lefty Stackhouse, an American touring pro of the 1930s and '40s, knocked himself out with a punch to the jaw after a missed putt. He once threw himself into a rosebush and thrashed around until he came out looking, as Dave Marr described it, as if he'd "fought a bunch of wildcats in a small room," and on another occasion after a poor round went out to the parking lot and destroyed his car, tearing off the windshield and doors and hurling around pieces of the engine. A contemporary of his named Ky Laffoon became so infuriated with his putter while driving from one tournament to another that he tied it to his door handle and watched it bounce along the road. More recently Jose Maria Olazabal broke his hand punching a hotel room wall at the U.S. Open after a round that displeased him.

Sergio Garcia has thrown his shoe. Tiger Woods has done a more than average amount of highly visible and audible club banging and cursing. Ben Crenshaw had to use his three iron on the greens in the 1987 Ryder Cup after destroying his putter.

Rhythm in golf is precarious, and rage is one of the things that most imperils it. It is also, in a game in which politeness is paramount, intrusively rude to others. A grave outbreak of rage can jeopardize a player's prize money and also his sponsorship contracts if his reputation becomes too sullied by it. But it is difficult to forever maintain poise or even to recover quickly from frenzied anger. Tom Watson watches the progress of a badly hit shot until the ball comes to a halt—partly to punish himself by taking in its complete awfulness but also to slow himself down and prevent himself from rushing after the ball and, in an effort to compensate for it, doing the same again. Ballesteros has deprived himself of meals after bad rounds. "You don't deserve to eat," he would tell himself. Greg Norman has pinched himself so often in self-punishment that his midsection was left an empurpled mess. Controlling rage is one of those acts of self-management, like giving up smoking or recovering from lost love, that, in the context of human history, can hardly be called heroic but which nevertheless requires a significant act of transcendence. One needs a powerful sense of equilibrium, perhaps an innate optimism, and a means of repressing the urge to be enraged without the rage staying locked within. One golf psychologist thinks that the emphasis on self-control in golf can perhaps be explained by its British origins, and that it can be healthier occasionally to explode. He says that the penalty strokes for breaking a club can be worth it if the rage is quickly dissipated. Perhaps through an act of leverage rage can be transformed into something else. Olazabal thinks it best not to kill it as it can be an aid to concentration. Above all, I think, a player needs the quality of acceptance. He should look at the bad shot as if from a distant star. But it is difficult and can be a slow process. Raymond Floyd thinks that the main reason most players don't enter their primes until their thirties is that it takes that long to find a way of dealing with anger.

But more treacherous mentally than anything else is the pressure of competitive golf. All tournaments are the stories not of a few hours but of nearly an entire week, and major tournaments in particular are a long haul, involving weeks of preparation, and are certainly among the most arduous experiences, at least mentally, in sport. The best players build their year around them. The courses are all extremely severe. A fifteen-handicapper playing a course set up for a championship from the back tees and with greens like the scalp of a skinhead would be unlikely to break one hundred in twenty attempts. On Augusta's greens during Masters week such a player would, as Peter Alliss has suggested, probably average four putts per hole. The player knows that everyone has to play the same course, but he also knows that a single errant shot can lose him hundreds of thousands of dollars and a victory. The atmosphere at a major championship is intense and vibrant and full of significance. You can feel it up to a mile away as you approach the course. In this atmosphere the player is utterly alone. He is unable to hide. He has no one to blame should there be a catastrophe. He fears degrading himself, not only before those immediately around him but also under the close scrutiny of millions watching on television around the world. Golf, like snooker, another game requiring extreme precision and executed from a starting position of complete stillness, is highly susceptible to pressure. The pressure is ever-present and increases inexorably if the player remains in contention. In golf the mind has ample time to fill with fear. Mind and body, which were united when the play was good, can instantaneously fragment into hundreds of component parts. The breath gets short, the muscles tighten, the mind cannot be stilled, the stomach turns, the heart races. Bobby Jones regularly lost up to eighteen pounds in the course of a major championship. It is even worse in the Ryder Cup, where to play badly is to risk not only loss and humiliation but also the grave disappointment of the captain, teammates, and the continent of fans, all of whose fates are bound up for those few days with the player's. Davis Love had been warned about how extreme an assault on the nerves is playing in the Ryder Cup, but nothing prepared him for what he felt as he faced an ostensibly simple short iron shot over water to the eighteenth green at the Belfry in 1993 when its failure or success would determine the outcome of the competition. "I couldn't breathe," he said. "There was no saliva in my mouth. It took all my strength not to kneel down in the fairway and throw up on myself." When Mark Calcavecchia lost the last four holes of his match to draw with Colin Montgomerie at Kiawah Island, he had to be taken to a medical tent and be given oxygen.

The first tee in a major championship can be a trauma, but the final few holes when the competition is close are of course many times worse. All golfers have felt this, even when the stakes are comparatively paltry. A Spanish friend of mine was playing in a tournament at his club, El Bosque in Valencia, the first prize for which was a watch. Playing off an eleven handicap, he was four over par on the eighteenth tee. He was hitting the ball extremely well and was full of confidence and knew that he was in a good, if not unassailable, position to win the tournament.

The eighteenth is a short par four that ends in a shallow green below the rising terraces of the clubhouse, on this day filled with people watching the players coming in. My friend was in the final group. He hit a splendid drive. As he walked up the fairway, he imagined the pleasure his brother would have when he bestowed the victory watch on him as a present. For his second shot he had a sixty-yard pitch to an elevated green. Word had spread about his fine round, and the members and their guests had gathered along the terrace railing to watch him complete his victory. He took his wedge from the bag, drew it back, and then buried it two inches behind the ball, which then ambled forward like a wheezing ancient short of a bunker in front of the green. His third nose-dived into the bunker, his fourth charged at ankle height over the green, and his fifth was hit fat and dribbled forward onto the fringe. He then three-putted for a quadruple bogey eight. The crowd watched fascinated by this self-immolation and then turned back to their drinks. He soon learned that one less shot would have won him the tournament outright, but that while his eight tied him for first, he placed second due to a rule that awarded first prize to the lower-handicap player in the event of a tie. He went out and sat in his car. He felt like eating it piece by piece in a grand, suicidal act of penance. Instead he beat the steering wheel with his fists and wept. It was the first time in his life that golf had reduced him to tears.

What happens in such circumstances to otherwise self-possessed and equable persons? The cardiovascular and other anatomical systems become deranged. The mind runs around like a rat in a maze. Concentration, control, and confidence unravel with increasing velocity until the player is a pitiable spectacle, turning as if on a spit over a fire of his own making. Such was the case at the Masters in 1996, when Greg Norman carried a six-shot lead into the final round and eventually finished five shots behind Nick Faldo. Watching on television in the clubhouse, Norman's Florida neighbor Nick Price finally turned away. "This is making me sick," he said.

Arnold Palmer, who often finished in a dazzling flurry of birdies and eagles to overtake the field and win, could also fall spectacularly. He let a seven-shot lead go over the final nine holes of the 1966 U.S. Open and then lost in a play-off the next day to Billy Casper. He had a two-shot lead going into the last hole at Augusta and hit a perfect drive. As he walked up the fairway, a friend called out from beyond the ropes, "Congratulations!" "Thanks," said Arnold. This small, premature exchange was enough to shatter his concentration. He hit his approach shot into the bunker to the left of the green, the succeeding shot into the bunker on the right, then came out and two-putted for a six, losing the following day in a play-off with Gary Player. The patina of assurance is so fragile, the door that leads down into a vortex so easily opened. A pro once told me that he had long harbored a grievance against another pro because of a malicious act of gamesmanship. He bided his time. One day they were playing the last day of a tournament together with his nemesis in the lead by three shots with four holes to play. On the fifteenth tee he played his card. "What are you going to say in your acceptance speech?" he asked his rival, who then produced a succession of double bogeys and went crashing down the leaderboard like a drunk down a flight of stairs.

To finish well a long and difficult labor in which the self is pitilessly exposed takes a different dimension of strength from what has been required up to that point. The urge to flee the task is great, and the ability to endure repeatedly in the face of this is another of the things that distinguishes the great players. It is the difference between Tom Wolfe bailing out before ending *The Bonfire of the Vanities* by contriving some newspaper reports to deal with the fates of his characters and, on the other hand, the magnificent and symphonic cascades of language with which James Joyce ended *Ulysses* and *Finnegans Wake*. He was at his best when the pressure was greatest and the stakes at their highest.

I once talked with a man who had worked with both Jean Van de Velde and Tiger Woods. Van de Velde's collapse was of course the most spectacular in a major championship since the beginning of mass television broadcasting. Needing a double bogey or better on the final hole to win the 1999 British Open at Carnoustie, he drove wildly to the right and then, in an abandonment of all sensible standards, elected a two iron to get out of the rough and clear the stream guarding the front of the green, hitting it again wildly right, into the stands. He got a drop into long rough and dumped the next one into the stream, took off his shoes and socks and rolled up his trousers, and climbed into the water as he contemplated the deranged notion of hitting the ball out, while all over the world viewers got down on their knees in front of their televisions to beg him not to do it, before finally deciding to drop a ball and take the penalty stroke. He hit this one into a greenside bunker, exploded out, then made a heroic putt for a triple bogey seven that got him into a four-hole play-off, which he lost. What happened to him? I asked his adviser. "For seventy-one holes he thought only of the shots he faced," he replied. "On the seventy-second tee he realized he could win the British Open. His entire system miswired." And Tiger? I asked. "He's always *in* the shot. He's very powerful in this sense. He makes his choice and then he executes. He does not allow extraneous thoughts about technique or his position in the tournament or the possible results of the shot to interfere with his making of the stroke he has decided upon. When he faced the twelve-foot putt he needed to make in order to stay alive in the sudden-death play-off against Ernie Els in the 2003 President's Cup, he saw the line and the distance, and the only thing that was in his head after that was making the stroke. Nothing more." At the time of writing, of the twenty-eight times Woods has been leading or tied for the lead after fifty-four holes, he has won twenty-six times. Of the other great major championship winners, both Hogan and Nicklaus were consistently strong at the close.

How is it done? When Bob Duval was leading a seniors' event after three rounds, he called his son David, then number one in the world, for advice. "What do you have to do to win, David?" he asked his son in a curious reversal of roles.

"You can't afford to think of what a win will mean to you," said David, who at the time was leading the Players' Championship. "You have to play your game one shot at a time. If you make some bogeys early, stay in the present. Does any of this sound familiar? Forget the last hole, the next hole, the eighteenth hole, or any other hole. *This* hole is the only hole. *This* shot is the only shot. And don't forget, the reason you're in the final group is that you're playing well."

Later that day, father and son each won his tournament.

A good young player setting out on the tour will almost certainly face a long period of failure before he ever begins to win anything important. Perhaps this is the hardest of all the tests presented by professional golf to a player who has been accustomed to winning regularly as an amateur. Jack Nicklaus and Tiger Woods began winning immediately, but the more common story is that of Justin Rose, who nearly won the British Open as a teenage amateur and then missed his first twenty-one cuts as a pro. He has since played superb golf often and was at one point leading the 2004 Masters, but he had to travel a hard and desolating road to get there.

Golf's apprenticeship is long, perhaps the longest in sport. Several of the greatest players labored in near anonymity for a decade before entering their period of glory. Ben Hogan went on the tour in 1932 and did not win anything at all until 1940. He won his first major in 1946. Bobby Jones entered the U.S. Open eleven times before he finally won it, his first major, in 1923. Chick Evans was a loser in the semifinals of the U.S. Amateur so often that he was moved to write a lyric about it.

I've a semi-final hoodoo, I'm afraid.

I can never do as you do, Jimmy Braid.

I've a genius not to do it,

I excel at almost to it,

But I never can go through it, I'm afraid.

He finally got to the finals in 1912 but was crushed seven and six by Jerry Travers and was so depressed he wandered off alone down a country road with the noise of Travers's victory party pouring from the clubhouse windows behind him. After a long while he came to a barn where he could hear music playing. A square dance was going on inside and he danced himself through the night into equanimity. But he still didn't win the championship until four years later. Tom Watson was thought to have insufficient nerve to win a major championship after collapses at the Masters and U.S. Open, but he eventually won five British Opens in nine years, as well as three other majors, beating Nicklaus toe-to-toe a few times with Nicklaus playing at his best. Someone in golf is always being asked, "What does it feel like repeatedly to have failed to win a major championship?"

A long apprenticeship can be demoralizing, but it may also be necessary. A golfer must almost certainly lose often to find the way to win. We learn to walk by failing. "It takes ten years to learn to write a sentence," according to the novelist Charles Newman, and after ten years it remains an activity largely carried out in the dark, failure a kind of ghost accompanying a writer line by line, year after year. A sentence, like a golf shot, is nearly always a miss or approximation of some kind. A gifted young golfer turning pro may hit the ground running, but he will almost always be felled brutally and repeatedly by the tour. He must learn hard lessons about his weaknesses and strengths and how to adapt to them, he must learn to think well, handle pressure, and find a way to win. But no matter how good he is and how successful he is at learning these things, he will still win rarely. Nicklaus in his best years won less than a quarter of the tournaments he entered. And even at the highest level the player fails with nearly every shot. "Ever tried. Ever failed. No matter. Try again. Fail again. Fail better," wrote Samuel Beckett, golfer and writer.

There finally comes the time when the great champion enters the era over which he will establish his ascendancy, when all the elements of his game come to fruition, when he displays those qualities of suppleness and courage and beauty that Solon praised in the first Olympic athletes. There are certain rounds, tournaments, and occasionally seasons when a great golfer's play is definitive of the best of himself and his time, when he is untouched and leaves all around him awed, when, as C.L.R. James wrote about Gary Sobers batting in Brisbane in 1961, "He seemed to be expressing a personal vision." In recent years, for example, there have been Ballesteros shooting sixty-five to beat Nick Price at Lytham in 1988, Greg Norman's final round at Sandwich in 1993, Tiger Woods at Augusta in 1997 or through the millennial season when he won three major championships. The mind in such cases seems entirely to possess the course and the game. The club feels light and the hole looks big. Time moves slowly. The path of the shot and the ball itself are vividly apprehended. The player feels strong, loose, and balanced and walks as though buoyed on a cloud. He may not go so far as to say it to himself, but he believes innately that he cannot miss. He is free of worry, and of thought. There is a wonderful, easeful singularity and simplicity to it all, the ball rising from the heart of the club, the putts rolling in, the ball doing just as the player wishes it to do, over and over.

Arnold Palmer described this feeling: "When I was at my best, I was always completely in the game. The concentration was automatic. Concentration comes out of a combination of confidence and desire. One year when I was still in college, I entered the Azalea Open, which was a professional tournament down in North Carolina. I stayed with some friends of mine who had a cottage there, and while we were having a few beers around the table the night before the tournament, one of them asked me what I was going to do the next day. I was to be in a threeball with two of the top five money winners that year. I suppose I had cause to be nervous, but I felt well. I said to my friend, 'I'll tell you what I'm going to do,' and I went through the entire eighteen holes, shot by shot. He laughed and I laughed, but then I went to bed and dreamed it all over again, the whole round of golf. And when I played the next day, I did exactly what I said I would do. I shot sixty-five. I never came out of that feeling the whole way around. I *loved* it. It was the same with the last round of the U.S. Open at Cherry Hills. I wasn't afraid of anything. I just saw where I wanted the ball to go and I put it there."

The trajectory of the career of a champion also has a downward arc. Nicklaus's trajectory has been longer than anyone else's, probably because his reserves of concentration were greater and because when he was younger, he had the foresight to play well within himself and schedule his season so as not to leave himself exhausted. But of course for him too the point of no return has arrived. As he said himself when he was fifty-four, "People have always said, 'Jack, I wish I could play like you.' Well, now they can."

Usually a great player lasts no longer than six or eight years at the top of the game. Why should this be? Golf is not sprinting, or jujitsu. There is some diminishment in strength and stamina with age, but it is not sufficient to be of great significance in a sport where these characteristics are less prominent. Yet most dominant players have ceased to be dominant by the age of forty. Often it's putting. Some subtlety of touch begins to fade, followed by belief, until the player has no idea of what will happen as he crouches over the ball. Toward the end of his competitive career Bobby Jones used to stand over putts and hear the pounding of his heart like the beating of a Lambeg drum, his whole field of vision washed over as though with a red dye. Hogan came to loathe putting. He once said while walking toward the practice green at Augusta, "And now for the blood bank," and once proposed that holes, and along with them putting, be eliminated from the game, the victor being the player who hit the most greens in regulation with the ball nearest to the pin. As he got older, he stood longer and longer over the ball on the greens, unable to move his hands.

Tony Jacklin arrived at the point where the finish of a round brought two sensations in rapid succession—first, relief that he would no longer have to putt that day, and second, dread that he would have to do so again the following day. Bernhard Langer had three breakdowns of the system with respect to putting, but somehow, through method and force of will, found his way back. Tom Watson, once one of the most confident putters ever in the game, arrived in his forties still striking the ball as well as anybody but found himself going into a spasm over short putts. It is traumatizing, and the player can receive wounds to the psyche from which he may never recover. The condition takes the form of paralysis, and when finally the move is made to strike the putt, the player has no control over or knowledge of what his hands, shoulders, and head are doing. Mark James stood over a putt late in a close match at the 1989 Ryder Cup and found himself paralyzed from the waist down. "What do I do now?" he thought as players, caddies, and spectators watched him in silence. He tried to walk away, but his feet wouldn't move. His feet had not yet properly got into position. Finally, he pushed with his shoulders, his hands moved, the ball was struck and against all probability went in. Brian Barnes, perhaps feeling the effects of the liquor store he then used to carry around in his bag, evidently holds the professional record for most putts on a single green, eleven, the final ten of them from within five feet. Some players suffer this anguish throughout their careers and therefore never win championships. Wild Bill Mehlhorn was one of the great ball-strikers of the twenties and thirties and once managed to shoot sixty-five in a competition while so drunk that he had to get his caddie to tee the ball for him so he wouldn't fall over. But he couldn't putt. He once six-putted in a tournament from ten feet. In another tournament he had a three-foot putt to tie for the lead, and after standing over it for a long time he whacked it off the green and into a bunker. One of his playing partners standing on the fringe of the green had to leap out of the way of the ball.

Arnold Palmer thinks that a champion's demise often has to do with fear. "You become a victim of yourself," he has said. "You play with confidence and win major tournaments, but then you're like the big home-run hitter who hits seventy home runs one season and then the following spring on the first day of the season he looks at the pitcher and thinks, 'Damn, I've got to hit seventy home runs again this year.' He tries to protect what he's done, and the doubts come in, and maybe that year he only hits ten home runs. In golf you know you can play the game, but you begin to think, 'I've got to keep the ball on the fairway,' or, 'I can't afford to three-putt.' Where you used to attack, now you're protecting. It all just gets fed into the diet and you find you're not winning tournaments like you used to do. Whether you win again at all depends on how well you handle this. But nobody escapes it. It's like death. If you hang around long enough, it's going to get you."

No one's decline from the top of the game has been as precipitous as Severiano Ballesteros's. The man the late English golf writer Peter Dobreiner described as "the great matador of golf" has retired from competition in his mid forties, having passed most of a decade hitting shots that would shame a fifteen-handicapper and only rarely making a cut. I watched him play a private game with Michael Jordan on a windy day in Spain in late 2004. He hit shockingly bad shots from everywhere, off the tee, from the fairway and the rough and on the greens, this player who won seventy-two tournaments, including five majors, and intimidated nearly everyone in golf throughout the 1980s. How has this happened? Like many professional golfers he has had trouble with his back. Perhaps for the past decade he has given the greater part of himself to his family, and while the wish to win may remain, the deep need to do so does not. Certainly money can no longer motivate him as he has earned enough on his own to keep several succeeding generations and also married into one of the richest families in Spain. He has also listened to so much conflicting technical advice that he may in some way have short-circuited, for what was once the freest and most majestic swing in golf now appears hemmed in by paranoia. He himself has spoken of bad and good golf in terms of mood, forces unknowable and beyond control, the good mood something that one can with all fervor and sincerity invite to come, but which nevertheless moves mysteriously and capriciously. "I had one mood from 1976 through 1986," he has said, "a mood of great confidence and optimism. I always felt aggressive, I always had a great deal of self-control, I always felt I would get good bounces. Then . . . I didn't feel so invincible. I was pessimistic. I believed that if something could go wrong, it would go wrong. I thought there was the devil in me. I said, 'Where has the confidence gone? Where has the optimism gone?' It hadn't left me. It was *inside* me, but I couldn't bring it out." Artists at times similarly speak of their works as mysteries. They themselves are not the progenitors of these works, but rather the transcribers. The work arrives from elsewhere and the artist records it. They try to tune themselves to stay open to these visions, they court muses and enact rituals to remain in contact, but beyond that there is nothing they can do. They cannot *create,* because the origin of the work is not in them. Bob Dylan once said, "Up to a time I used to write subconsciously. The songs existed somewhere, I heard them and wrote them down. I never had any fear that they would stop. But then one day I took a step and the lights went out. I had amnesia. I couldn't do it anymore. I tried all kinds of ways to get it back, but I couldn't get to the source. . . . Then I met a man in New York who put my mind and my hand and my eye together, and I found I could do consciously what before I did subconsciously. I don't know how long I'll stay connected . . ."

Ezra Pound believed that people have been born with an allotted word hoard, and because of this he stayed silent for long periods to conserve his words and thereby have some left to spend when he was old. Perhaps athletes each have a finitude of desire, and that with each competitive effort they draw on this bank until the reserves are spent. In golf it could perhaps be said that Tom Weiskopf, for example, was granted a lesser amount of this than Jack Nicklaus. Ballesteros had two phases, or moods, of winning with élan, and when he looked for a third, it could not be found. Samuel Beckett yearned nostalgically for decades for that time of explosive productivity during which he wrote *Waiting for Godot* and *Endgame* and his trilogy of novels, writing all day and drinking all night, the supply of language seemingly never-ending. But it played itself out and the words came to him in diminishing numbers, something out of which he made an aesthetic in itself, but which nevertheless became a kind of anguish, his hand, he said, drifting across the table to his closed exercise book, stalling, and then withdrawing without a word being recorded. If he succeeded in writing a sentence, his mind would usually howl, "That's a lie!"

Athletes, perhaps like women of great beauty, know that the period of their glory has a limit. But this does not mean that all can accept this with ease. When Arnold Palmer at nearly seventy went around his home course in Latrobe, Pennsylvania, in sixty-three, he couldn't stop himself from dreaming that somewhere within him there was perhaps one more victory. Athletes give themselves in mind and spirit and body to competing and winning. It is what constitutes their identity. It is intense, all-engrossing, elemental, and when it goes, it must leave a painful vacancy. "I am happiest when I am in the hunt for the title," Ballesteros has said. "I am like the gambler. The great moment is not when the roulette wheel has finished spinning, and the gambler knows whether he has won or lost. The great moment comes when the wheel is spinning, and he does not yet know the outcome. That's what I live for." Older champions have been accustomed for so long to turning their minds toward the hunt that when winning is no longer possible, there is a loss of meaning. "I can live without playing the Masters," Jack Nicklaus has said. "But the really satisfying time is the three weeks leading up to the Masters when I'm preparing for it."

The tour can become a way of life, competing addictive. Many professional golfers, like boxers, go on when they can no longer compete as equals. But the time finally comes for all of them when it is over, when everything associated with tournament golf is behind them. Some may find a way of enjoying this, others not.

"Don't ever get old," said Ben Hogan in 1971 when he withdrew from a tournament after eleven holes due to fatigue and pain. He'd hit three balls into a ravine on the par three fourth, hurt his knee trying to hack the last of them out, and made a nine on the hole. He went out in forty-four and double-bogeyed ten and eleven.

When Chick Evans was well into his eighties, my father received a Christmas card from him that included one of his lyrics:

> My memory pauses for pleasing retrospection of all the
>   marvelous
> dreams, remembering the best and forgiving the rest.
>
> The Masterpieces, long have I worked back through the past
>   on them; now
> the world seems deaf because no one listens; I feel pained at
>   times.
>
> We all face something that others cannot know; all Earth's
>   peoples share
> the wait for Death to bring the slow answers; Life's night
>   comes when
> hope is dead; 'til then grows the doubt that never dies.

Perhaps this is old age for most people, or perhaps this particular combination of pain and doubt and isolation happens during an old age carrying with it the memory of great deeds long past and mostly forgotten, at least by others.

Thinking of this process, this journey through time made by the champion golfer—the great labor, the long wait, the display of imagination and nerve and will, the isolation, the exposure of self, the fall—the player who comes most frequently into my mind is Ben Hogan. It is not that he was the best. I think the question of who was the best is without meaning. Nor is it that he was prototypical, for no one was at all like him. It is that, with his silence, his search for perfection, and his ferocious determination, he was the most elementally expressive of golf as a technique and golf as competition. It is that he was somewhere near the square root of all that goes into defining these things. I never saw him play at his best or even saw him interviewed. I vaguely remember watching on television when he was in contention after the third round of the 1967 Masters, but he was fifty-five then and he faded before the final nine. What I know of him comes only from quotation and anecdote. But from this he seems the most mysterious of professional golfers, his life utterly covert and his golf a spectacle of naked will. He was driven by a search for perfection and, according to Dave Marr, got closer to it "than any man who ever played the game." Nicklaus, among others, thought him the finest striker of the ball he'd ever seen. A journalist watching him practice four-wood shots reported that the caddy 230 yards out in the field never had to take more than five paces to the right or left to collect the balls. He often went through thirty-six-hole final days on fiercely difficult courses in major championships never missing a fairway or a green, and never speaking. He thought that on average he hit only one perfectly pure shot per round, and that if he could average three or four, he might shoot in the fifties. He once had a dream in which he made seventeen holes in one and a two. "When I woke up," he said, "I was so goddamned mad."

What drove him? When asked, he said that he wanted to make enough money so as not to be a burden to his widowed mother. But could it also have been anger at the world, some need for vengeance? Some writers write, perhaps, and painters paint for this primeval reason. Céline, Knut Hamsun, Goya. Bob Dylan reached heights of eloquence driven by venom. What part of Shakespeare was Hamlet? Hogan had ample enough causes to be angry at the world. "I had a tough day all my life," he said. He grew up poor. He was in the room when his father killed himself with a .38 revolver shot to the head. He was small and was beaten around the caddy yard in Fort Worth, Texas, until finally he beat up somebody bigger than him. He worked demonically on his game but it was a long time before he won anything. Year after year he went out on the tour and came back broke. This frustrated him terribly. For a while during the winter tour in California he and his wife survived mainly on oranges they picked from the trees, and when they were down to their last eight dollars, he came out of his motel room to find his car up on blocks and all the wheels stolen. He stood beating his fist into the wall. When finally he began to win major championships and dominate the tour, his car was hit head-on by a bus on a narrow bridge on a foggy morning and his leg was smashed. Obituaries were read out on the radio, but he pulled through it. Letters arrived from all over the country, and Byron Nelson said it was the first time this solitary, taciturn man realized he had friends. He went back out on the tour a year later and continued winning, but with a severely restricted schedule because of poor circulation in his leg. In 1953 he entered six tournaments and won five, three of them majors, including a win at the British Open at Carnoustie that remains legendary in Scotland. He might have made the Grand Slam had he entered the PGA.

On the course he was intense, austere, laconic, enveloped inviolably in concentration. There was no humor or evident joy in his golf. Frivolity appalled him. He told his friend Claude Harmon that Harmon had a good chance to win the U.S. Open at Winged Foot because he was a good player and also the resident pro and therefore knew the course better than anyone, but that he wouldn't do it because he played what Hogan called "jolly golf"—which for him was golf with conversation. He barely noticed a hole in one Harmon made when they were playing together at the Masters. George Fazio knocked in an eight iron for an eagle in front of his hometown crowd when playing with Hogan, and though the gallery went wild and play was delayed, Hogan had no memory of it after the round. He hadn't a concept of a relaxing day on the golf course. "I play golf with friends but we don't play friendly golf," he said. When invited to play a round with the king of Belgium, he said, "I don't play golf while on holiday." Golf was war, with the course, with the competition, and with himself, and he had to win. You prepared for this war with long and punishing labor, and from this there was no escaping. When a young pro asked him for advice, he said, "Go dig it out of the ground like I did." Bad shots made him want to vomit. In particular he loathed the hook, which plagued him in his early years. "It's like a rattlesnake in your pocket," he said. Hogan passed through many people's lives in his long career. He astounded spectators and players with his power and precision, his self-containment and ferocity. But it seems he remained unknown.

Hogan was, with Vardon, Jones, Hagen, Palmer, and Nicklaus, an epoch-maker in the history of golf. They were dominant in their time and they all moved the game on in some way. As nearly everyone who has ever heard of golf knows, we entered the era of Tiger Woods shortly after he turned professional in 1996. He has moved the game on in the revenue he generates, the global spread of his fame, the quality and intensiveness of his physical conditioning and his preparation for major tournaments, his invention of new shots, his manner of organizing his season, the strength of his mind, his belief in himself, and the miraculous way he has played the game. He has stepped off his throne, perhaps just for a while, but many who have been watching golf for a long time would say that the game has never seen anything so gloriously masterful as his play from 1999 to the late spring of 2003.

He turned pro in 1996, but his coming, like some astronomical phenomenon, had long been foreseen, for he has been the youngest to do virtually anything of merit in golf. He was an infant prodigy who demonstrated his swing on national television when he was two. When he was three, he shot forty-eight for nine holes. By the time he was eight he was regularly breaking eighty. He taped a newspaper clipping onto his bed while still a child listing Jack Nicklaus's earliest achievements, starting with his first breaking seventy when thirteen. The article is still there, as too are Nicklaus's records.

Woods won three consecutive U.S. Junior championships, succeeded directly by three U.S. Amateurs, one of the most grueling tournaments in golf. He won the first major championship he entered as a pro, the 1997 Masters, by twelve shots, being the youngest ever winner of this tournament and breaking its scoring records. He is the youngest player to complete the career Grand Slam and is the only player in the history of golf to have won all four of the modern majors in succession. He currently holds the scoring records in all of them. He passed from Infant Prodigy to Boy Wonder and, at an age when most professionals are just entering their prime, is already a veteran.

Like most golf stories, his is a story of father and son. Earl Woods placed the six-month-old Tiger in a high chair in his garage so he could watch as his father hit golf balls into a net, the rhythm of the swing and the thwack of impact drifting down into his subconscious and the memory system of his muscles like medicine drip-fed into a vein. Later, when he was a teenager, his father would walk along beside him on the course, occasionally sneezing or dropping the bag in the midst of his swing. He kept it up round after round until finally the boy could take anything his father tried on him, smiling eerily amidst a bombardment of rattled coins, coughs, and midswing exclamations. His control is now acute. He can halt his downswing in a millisecond as if he's pressed pause on a video. A fellow pro saw him do it on the eighteenth tee in a tournament he was leading by a shot. Someone called out "Tiger!" when he was in the middle of his downswing and he stopped cold. "How does he do that," asked the pro, "with the club so close to the ball? It's moving at 125 miles per hour."

When he came out on the tour, he finished sixtieth in his first tournament, then eleventh, fifth, and third. He won his first tournament as a pro, the Las Vegas Invitational, shooting a sixty-four on the Sunday to catch Davis Love and then beat him in a play-off. Two weeks later he won again and in April won the Masters. Within months of turning pro he had become the game's protagonist, and everyone knew they were seeing something they hadn't seen since the arrival of Nicklaus.

Nicklaus declared him a more complete player than he had been, and quicker to develop. His length, of course, was immediately apparent, the power deriving from a conditioned strength but also from a supreme athleticism. He can run one hundred meters in eleven seconds. After watching him hit a two iron 292 yards through the air, the English golf journalist David Davies did some calculations and announced that a course would have to be 8,750 yards long for it to be a legitimate par seventy-two for him. He was wild off the tee, but he could hit shots few others would dare try and most could not even imagine, and also brought new shots into the game—punched two irons and three woods off the tee, a big sweeping hook with a three wood that ran nearly as long as it flew, the three-wood chip from the side of the green. He demonstrated an extraordinary capacity for the great shot and, with grinding repetition, the great putt. At the 2000 PGA he was a shot behind on the fifteenth green facing a complicated fifteen-foot putt for par while the leader, Bob May, had a four-footer for birdie. Former USGA president Frank Tatum was watching on television. "Tiger stalks the putt like I've never seen a putt stalked before, but there's a total calm about him. The camera is following him. I feel as if I'm right in his eyes. Arnold Palmer had that same quality. He made TV alive. Anyway, Tiger makes, May misses, Tiger wins his third straight major. I knew that if I had been in that spot, I would've been thinking about defeat. The only thing Tiger was thinking about was making the putt."

He played with fearlessness, complete presence of mind, and a quiet but brutal competitiveness, each slight filed away, ready to be answered. Notah Begay was on the President's Cup team the year that Vijay Singh's caddy wore a hat with "Tiger who?" stitched onto the back. "It pissed Tiger off," said Begay, "and that's the last thing you want to do." They played the singles against each other on the Sunday, and on the fourth Tiger made Singh putt out, even though he'd already made bogey and Singh had only an eight-footer for a birdie. He wanted, said Begay, to annoy Singh, and thus to make him play better. "Why would Tiger want Vijay to play better?" said Begay. "Because Tiger wants to beat Vijay at his best. Vijay at his best is going to bring out Tiger at his best, and Tiger at his best is the best in the world. If he wins, it's only going to help Tiger somewhere down the road. To get into another player's head like that you've got to be extremely perceptive and observant, which Tiger is. He sees everything and files it away. . . . He beat Vijay that day two and one. He's not going to beat the Vijays of the world every time, but he will win more often than not."

The love of the game and the mental control may be bequests from his father, but this other dimension, it seems, derives from his mother. "Old man is soft," Tida Woods said to Tom Callahan, author of the fine book *In Search of Tiger*. "He cry. He forgive people. Not me. I don't forgive anybody." She advised Tiger, "Go after them, kill them. Go for their throats. Don't let them up. When you're finished, now it's sportsmanship."

By the end of the 2000 season Tiger was deeply in the minds of the corpus of the tour, debilitatingly. Davis Love said that there was no physical reason why a number of players, Mickelson, Els, or Duval, for example, couldn't play as well. But "Tiger's better mentally and knows it. He knows we know it too." Ernie Els played with him in the final round of the 2000 U.S. Open at Pebble Beach. For 138 years Old Tom Morris's win by thirteen shots at the British Open was the largest margin of victory in a major. Tiger beat it by two. "If that's not perfect, I don't know what is," said Els afterward. "He never got ahead of himself. If you want to see a guy win the U.S. Open playing perfectly, you've just seen it. . . . I don't know what more there is to be said about him. We've been talking about him for the last two years. I guess we'll be talking about him for the next twenty. When he's on, we don't have much of a chance." Nick Price, forty-three at the time, said, "I feel sorry for the younger guys. Basically, I've had my day."

It began to seem as if players felt they were not entitled to beat him. At the 2002 Masters, Singh and Els got close to him on the back nine but then hit their balls into the water on the par fives, Singh repeatedly. When Tiger came back from his knee operation in early 2003, he won three of the first four tournaments he entered, winning for the fourth consecutive time at Bay Hill by eleven shots, playing the final round in the rain with food poisoning, vomiting twice, it was reported, on the course. "Tiger's only thinking about Tiger," Nick Faldo said afterward. "And everybody else is only thinking about Tiger."

Tiger focused on Nicklaus early and has kept him in his mind since. It's been said that he was familiar with the word *Nicklaus* before he knew it was a name, so often did his father say it. Nicklaus was a kind of concept to him and has remained so. "If you aspire to greatness, you have to have a clear picture of greatness," he has said. They first met at an exhibition at the Bel-Air Country Club in Los Angeles when Tiger was sixteen and Nicklaus fifty-one. Tiger displayed an array of shots for the gallery and Nicklaus called out, "Tiger, when I grow up, I want to have a swing as beautiful as yours."

Tiger won three U.S. Amateurs to Nicklaus's two and started winning both regular tour events and majors at a quicker rate. But still far off in the distance are Nicklaus's eighteen majors, and the even more unassailable thirty-seven top twos, forty-six top threes, and seventy-two top tens in majors. Can he do it? Tom Callahan asked Nicklaus if it would distress him if it happened. "No, I'll be happy for him," he said. "I'll be even happier for golf. Bobby Jones was great. My coming along didn't diminish him. Poor Tiger. You know, I never tacked Jones's records up on my bedroom wall. The first time I thought—even thought—about his records was when I won the British Open at St. Andrews in 1970 and somebody said, 'That's your tenth major, Jack. Only three more to tie Jones.' This kid wins his first Masters and everybody says, 'Seventeen more to go, Tiger.' But he can handle it, I'm sure he can. It's his turn." The records are inscribed in his consciousness. He knows them better even than Nicklaus does. He told Callahan, "I've always studied him. Warming up on the practice tee, do you know why I start off with an eight iron? Because he does. And I still look at his records."

What can stand in his way of surpassing them? Several things are possible. He swings hard at the ball and with violently fast hip action, so that it would seem to someone as unknowledgeable as myself that there is very little margin for error in the timing. This is compounded by his lowering of the body on the downswing, requiring him to rise again just before impact so that he can get back into position. I wonder if he can carry such an uneaseful swing into his late thirties and forties. And his putting could go, like anybody's.

But I think the threat to his reaching the fullness of his potential over the next twenty years is more likely to come, if it comes at all, from within him, from a diminution of hunger. Corporate executives and their advertisers could do it. They continue to crawl all over him looking for ways to exploit his talent, his looks, his intensity, his blackness. They specialize in the appropriation of the engaging and substantial and individualistic, and then spitting them out. Iggy Pop, Labi Siffre, John Lennon, and Pablo Picasso have been used to sell cars. Photographs of political protest have been used to sell vacations. Smirnoff even tried to use the famous iconographic portrait of Che Guevara to sell its vodka, but the rights were not for sale. The cynicism of the advertising world now runs so deep that it appears they are more interested in draining things of their meanings, of turning authenticity and passion into what they think of as irony and chic, than they are even in selling their products. It could sicken the person thus used. It is lucrative, but violating. Certainly Tiger Woods is as commercially exploitable as anyone now living, and he would be wise to be cautious, as I imagine he is. His hunger to win could also be threatened by satiation, a wish for privacy and freedom of movement, or concentration on a family or a woman. Perhaps some of this affected him during his second year on the tour, a mediocre time by his standards during which he often, I thought, looked sullen. It is said that Michael Jordan advised him that the most precious asset that he had was his love for the game and that to protect it he should leave the business to others.

As I write, he is not the supreme and inviolable presence he was. The victories have lately been arriving more seldomly and he has competed in a long string of majors without a win. He seems to have difficulty putting together four high-caliber rounds, or of making something happen when he needs it. There is a ghost, it seems, in his head, perhaps a species of the fear Arnold Palmer says is the plague of champions. It is certainly also true that in 2000 the other players realized that if they were to have a chance at all, they would have to find a way of raising their games, and all the leading ones have done so. He is now playing against a stronger, longer hitting, fitter, and more concentrated and purposeful field than he once was, largely because of the standards he himself set, with a game that is marginally off. Many theories have been advanced—his knee is still bothering him, he should never have got rid of his coach Butch Harmon, the glut of trophies and fame and money have dimmed his interest. Some blame the arrival in his life of his exceptionally beautiful Swedish wife, Elin. He himself says he's changing his swing. "He accomplished so much in such a short period of time," says Arnold Palmer, "and his life now is changing, as lives do. I think he has to go home, sit down calmly, and analyze himself. What is the bottom line? What is important to him? Where does he want to go? How much of himself is he now willing to dedicate to the game, and how much to other spheres of his life?"

I think ultimately his strength is that he is driven not only by a hunger to win, but also by a sense of destiny. Jack Nicklaus's records stayed taped to his wall long after he left home. He knows that it is a long story to get there, and though he may never arrive, he wants to see the journey through to the end, and to perhaps leave his mark in time. He is, as C.L.R. James said of Sobers, "expressing a personal vision."

There were those with a limited knowledge of the game who thought it boring when he was winning so much, and by such large margins. They do not realize how difficult and susceptible to chance the game is, how seldom are anyone's victories, even Nicklaus's or his, or how fragile any player's grasp of the game can be, even the best. I love to see him win. Like Palmer and Ballesteros, he plays an exuberant, thrilling, and explosive version of the game, and I think it a great fortune to be able to see it for, as Ernie Els has said, probably no one has ever played like that. He loves striking the ball, the imagined shot made real, a kind of signature in the air. There is an optimism about him, and a quality of radiance he projects when the game is good. He ignites people's imaginations and spirits. They feel a familiarity with him, so that for the galleries he is Tiger as Palmer was Arnie or Ballesteros Seve, while Hogan, for example, remained Hogan.

Yupa Poosorn, a lady Thai caddy, drew Rodney Pampling of Australia for the Johnnie Walker Classic at the Alpine Golf Club near Bangkok. Her family are rice farmers, but she loves golf, and above all else she wanted to see Tiger Woods, who was also competing in this tournament. "I prayed to the spirit and promised to bring it two chickens if Rodney Pampling made the cut and I saw Tiger Woods." As it happened, Pampling not only made the cut, he was paired in the final round with Tiger. Yupa Poosorn was extremely nervous all morning, but on the first tee Tiger came over and introduced himself and smiled at her and joked with her through a kind of sign language, and by the fourth hole, she said, she had calmed down. But it was nevertheless her one big day in golf. "I am so proud that Tiger is Thai," she said. "He is a very strong man. His body is definitely American, but his eyes are Thai. His smile is Thai. I promised the spirit that if I can ever be near Tiger Woods again, I will give it a whole pig."

6

.

Marooned with
Brigitte Bardot

When my friend rang from *Esquire* magazine to ask me what golf story I might like to write, I told him that I would like to play a round with Arnold Palmer. He said that sounded fine, and so I wrote a letter stating my case to "Arnold Palmer, Latrobe, Pennsylvania," but the game couldn't be arranged at that time and I wrote about other things. However, fifteen months later and just before New Year's, 1993, I got word from Pennsylvania that if I still wanted to play golf with Mr. Palmer, I was to be at the first tee of the Bay Hill Club in Orlando, Florida, on January 12.

I arrived three days early with a bad back and nearly nauseous with nerves. There had been a time when he was the second person in golf for me, after my father. I followed him around during his

practice rounds when he came to Chicago for the Western Open and watched his progress on the tour, perpetually, it seemed, on the edge of my seat. The idea then of actually playing golf with him was the sort of idle notion boys entertain themselves with before going to sleep. Like punching out the local thug. Or being marooned somewhere with Brigitte Bardot. Now I was at Bay Hill and it was about to happen. His name and face were everywhere there because he is the club's owner. Palmer winning the Masters. Palmer and Jack Nicklaus. Palmer and a few presidents. I stayed in the club's hotel and never left the grounds the entire time I was there, playing two practice rounds, putting, staying out on the range until it was dark. I saw him once at breakfast at a big table with friends and then later on his own prowling around a putting green at the back of the range like a bear in a cage. I didn't approach him. "What's it like to play with him?" I asked Jim Deaton, the head pro. "The first time I played with Mr. Palmer," he said, "I couldn't feel my thumbs for the first eleven holes. I hardly said anything at all because I kept rehearsing everything in my mind before I said it so I'd get it right."

The night before the round I lay on the floor in my room doing exercises for my back. I heard an irregular series of faint clicks outside, and I went onto the balcony to have a look. It was around midnight. The day had been cloudy, but a huge V-shaped fissure had opened in the sky to reveal a full moon and a knee-high white mist clinging to the bases of the palm trees and drifting along the ground. On the practice green below me, four teenage boys were having a putting contest. They looked incorporeal in the moonlight and mist. Just beyond them was the first tee. What was to happen to me there the next day at 12:20? Would I move the ball sideways three yards back between my legs? Would the driver fly out of my hands on the backswing? The father of a friend of mine was once invited to an outing at a club he had never played at before and, on the first tee, before a crowd of waiting golfers, had swung and missed twice. On his third attempt the ball dribbled forward twenty yards to the ladies' tee. He then turned to his gallery, solemnly shook his head, and said, "Tough course." At least I would have a line in the event of a disaster.

The next morning I went out early and played five holes badly. "Please not today," I whispered after each ballooned, blocked, and topped shot. I ran back to change my shirt and then over to the practice range. I got a few degrees of coordination back and then heard the starter announce through a loudspeaker, "First group of the shoot-out to the tee, please—Mr. Palmer, Mr. Damron, Mr. Mitchell, Mr. Dorman, and Mr. O'Grady." Arnold Palmer came down the steps from the pro shop, put on a straw hat, and walked over to the first tee. So did players coming off the ninth and eighteenth greens, everyone from the practice putting green, several from the driving range and swimming pool, caddies, waiters, club attendants, assistant pros, and a number of people in the middle of their lunches. I did not turn around to see how many there were, but from the way the skin was crawling on my back it felt like a multitude.

All four of my playing partners hit good, long drives into the heart of the fairway. Palmer's ball took off from the face of his large, metal-headed driver as if out of the mouth of a cannon and sailed into the atmosphere out of the range of my sight. I heard applause and a few whoops. I was last. My chest felt as if it were in flames. Golf bags, tee markers, and the trees up the fairway all looked out of proportion and shimmering, as if in a malign dream. I bent over to tee the ball up, looked along the ground, and there, just a few feet away, was Arnold Palmer, the great hero-warrior of my childhood. I could see his white Nike shoes, his sharply creased trousers, the powerful, veined forearms and blacksmith's hands, the fingers round and surprisingly short, like chipolatas. How had I come to be in this position? My hands were shaking so badly that the ball clattered on the tee like teeth in a cold wind. Above me, as if from the clouds, I heard him speak. "Take it easy," he said softly. "We're just here for an afternoon of golf. Enjoy yourself."

I stood up, looked, I suppose, imploringly at the ball, and tried to stay intact as I took my swing. The ball came off the clubface a little to the inside of center, climbed over a tree that guarded the slight dogleg, and settled down on the left side of the fairway, seventeen yards behind Arnold Palmer's. Never had I struck a golf shot invested with such turmoil.

I watched his back as he strode down the fairway. Winner of seven major titles over six years. At sixty-three the fourth-highest money-earner in all of sport. Possibly the most widely admired and trusted man in America. He would play that day in a way that reminded me of the games I had played with fellow caddies as a teenager—free and easy, laughing a lot, going full out for everything, a little angry at himself sometimes but also visibly loving the feeling of the ball being struck by the club. He still flailed at it with a violent, corkscrewing lunge. His drives carried 275 yards and I don't recall him missing a fairway with any of them. On a par three where I was using a three iron, I noticed that he had hit a six.

Our fiveball was one of around eight competing against each other that day, with each player throwing $30 into a pot for the winning team and the best three scores on each hole counting. By the time we came to the sixteenth, a par five, we were three over as a team and out of the hunt. Arnold hit a two-iron second over the water into some thick grass on the front fringe of the green. When he half-fluffed the chip, he winced as though someone had prodded him in the ribs, then said to the sky, "If I knew how to play that shot, I'd have won four more U.S. Opens." It occurred to me that I would be unlikely to hear that again on a golf course.

Just two holes left then. I could already feel the round slipping away like a passing dream and I longed to hold on to it. I had played with a moderate solidity and was eight over through sixteen, but then cracked up on the next, a long par three on which I hit two balls into the water and finished with a six. They were really hideous shots. I got a little round of applause from Arnold on the next, however, when I hit a four wood out of the rough and over water that landed next to the pin and stopped on the fringe of the green. He hit an eight iron for his second and finished one over for the day. I got a par for an eighty-three.

We headed for the clubhouse. Scott Hoch sped by on his own in a buggy. Arnold stopped to talk for a while with two teenagers and then went inside. We sat at a round table in the men's locker room and had three rounds of beers. I was so elated I felt I could have drunk vats of it. Andy Bean came in wearing long, white socks and pressed Bermuda shorts. He was carrying two framed photographs he wanted Arnold to sign for some friends. Arnold smiled, said, "Sure," and, as he wrote his name, said to Bean, "You're not playing golf in shorts, are you?" Bean is a large, evidently amiable, and relaxed man who won eleven times on the U.S. tour and played twice in the Ryder Cup, but in this moment he looked like a truant caught on his way out of a sweet shop. "Well . . . ahhh . . . just, you know, trying to get some sun on the legs . . . very white, the legs, after the winter . . . ," he said, then drifted away. Arnold waved and wished him well. He is gracious, easy, and attentive in company, but also has a formidable natural authority. I would not like to cross him. The English television commentator Peter Alliss, against whom Arnold had once competed in the Ryder Cup, interviewed him at Augusta, having decided to attack him for taking a place there without having a chance to win. Arnold answered the charge patiently, explaining about the tradition at the Masters and the gallery's sense of it. But Alliss wouldn't let it go, asking him if it didn't embarrass him to play so poorly at such a great championship, to be an old man taking the place of a younger, more deserving player. "Well, it could be worse," said Arnold. "At least I'm not running around after people trying to interview them."

We talked about a lot of things through the late afternoon—Hogan, Snead, his victory in the U.S. Amateur—"the one I am most proud of, I think"—the sixty-five he shot while still in college at the Azalea Open, the fears that beset champion athletes and his rivalry with Jack Nicklaus—"still as fierce as ever." Snead had in his view the best swing he had seen—"the most fluid, natural, and authentic." Hogan, whom he had supplanted as the dominant force in golf, couldn't understand him, it seems. "I arrived at Augusta in 1958 very tired. I'd just been in two hard battles over the previous weeks. I played a practice round with Hogan, very poorly, and afterwards in the locker room, I heard him say, 'What's that guy Palmer *doing* here?'" He won that year, his first of four Masters championships.

He was intelligent, unrestrained, and interesting about these and other matters, but the subject that seemed to stir him most was his father. Years after his father's death and decades after he himself had become heroic to so many people, he was still clearly awed by him, a tough, compact steelworker and club pro from western Pennsylvania with a foreshortened foot. "My father was one of the strongest men I ever met," he said. "He could do ten pull-ups with either arm and go practically all day if he used both. He was a severe disciplinarian and a great man for manners, but above all he had respect for other people. He told me that if I wanted to go to sleep with a clear conscience, I should treat everyone I came across as if I myself were that person. It's a simple enough principle, but maybe it could be forgotten if you were tired or had a bad round. But he'd driven very deeply into me the idea that everyone has their story and that you must take them as they come and care about them. Anything else is undeserving of respect. Because of the way he raised me I don't think there was much chance of me going off the rails or acting like a big shot, but if I had, I know he would have been there to make me see sense. He was tough. For a long time I didn't think he believed I could play golf. I had won the U.S. Amateur, several pro tournaments, and the Masters before he congratulated me. It was after the U.S. Open at Cherry Hills and he said, 'Nice going, boy.' I thought the world had come to an end."

We went out onto the golf course to have some pictures taken for the article I was to write. The photographer placed us nose to nose, as if to suggest two boxers promoting a fight. We had to hold this pose for a long time. "This would be a lot easier if you were a pretty girl," said Arnold as he looked into my eyes. He wrote a note to my father, then small and enfeebled in his bed in Chicago. His wife called him then on his cell phone and he told me he had to go. I watched him walk into the gathering darkness, hands in his pockets, checking the conditions of his trees, whistling lightly, I thought, as he rounded a corner, a driven, successful, yet unpretentious man. That was it then, my most memorable day on a golf course.

I went back to London and sent my father the note. He was about to become eighty-eight years old. He'd had a triple-bypass operation ten years earlier and finally retired from dentistry in his seventy-ninth summer. He had a dark view of retirement, made worse, it seemed, in his mind in the case of his particular profession. Once when we were in a hotel together in London, we stood in the hallway of an upper floor and watched a rotund, elderly man listing slowly from side to side as he made his way toward the door to his room, elbows and trouser seat shining on his pin-striped suit, shoelace undone. Perhaps he was a resident, perhaps a perpetual solitary traveler. The late afternoon shadows fell on him. "Retired dentist," said my father before we moved away. The bypass surgery invigorated him so much that in his first year of retirement he played up to three rounds of golf, and sometimes more, per week. When he was seventy-nine, he was four over par after fifteen holes on his home course and needed to finish three over for the difficult final three par fours in order to shoot his age. He went bogey, bogey, double bogey, for eighty. Then, the following year, he began, it seemed, slowly to evaporate. His hands and face became skeletal. Sometimes he looked both haunted and bewildered, as though he feared something bad might be coming to him but could not understand why this should be. He had the same physical expectations he'd had more than thirty years earlier, but the body would not react as it had. "Getting old," he said, "is without compensations." He walked a few times per week to the school playing fields to hit nine irons from the same spot I had used as a teenager, but he ceased going to the golf course. I tried several times to get him to come with me when I visited him, but he wouldn't shift. "If I swung a golf club now, I'd fall over," he said.

Finally, when he was eighty-six, I persuaded him to come out as a spectator for a round I was to play with three friends of his. He stayed sitting in his buggy with his eyes shaded by the brim of his hat until the twelfth hole, a par three, when he asked to hit a shot. He hadn't struck a golf ball in at least three years. The emaciation had now advanced so far that his flesh seemed like a fine layer of gauze over his bones. He looked terribly frail as he stood alone on the tee lining up the shot. I yearned for him to at least get the ball airborne. He took no practice swing. The club came back with a familiar little hitch near the top of the backswing, then the right knee kicked in and the right elbow stayed tight to the ribs as he accelerated smoothly and classically, the head down and behind the ball as he hit into and through the shot—all those elements of controlled abandon he had instructed me in years before. It was as though an inner ghost were moving the derelict frame. He hit it thin, but it ran up to the edge of the green.

7

·

The Mind, and Its Absence

"Pros," Tom Watson has said, "used to hunt in packs." They drove from tournament to tournament, sometimes sharing cars, sometimes pulling trailers. They might have a barbecue and a few beers in a clearing and then hit the bars. Jimmy Demaret once led a few pros to a nightclub where fellow competitor Don Cherry was singing and from a drinks-laden table rolled golf balls onto the stage. They loaned each other money and exchanged clubs and advice. They rarely sought counsel from outside their milieu.

A leading tournament professional now might employ the services of a physiotherapist, a dietitian, a biomechanical specialist, a stylist, a club technician, a swing coach, a psychologist, and a PA for logistics, as well as the more traditional employees, such as manager and caddy. Pros have a lot of people around them now, but few are their peers.

I've wondered about this assemblage from time to time, how its individual members fit together, how effective they are, but I never came into contact with one until a friend of mine named Steve Carr told me about Dr. Paul Lagier, mind specialist to numerous South American and European pros.

"I went to see him for a couple of days in Seville," Steve told me.

"And?"

"For fifteen years I've played off four. Within two months I was down to two."

"That's amazing," I said. "What was the message?"

There was a pause.

"You won't get it," he said then.

"Try," I said.

He rubbed forefinger and thumb together and looked toward the sky as if trying to describe the subtle flavor of a good wine.

"It's all about . . . *feel*," he said finally.

I had no idea what that meant, but I contacted Dr. Lagier and traveled to Seville to see him. We sat in the clubhouse bar of the Club Zaudin, diagrams, a medical textbook, and a laptop computer on the table before us.

"Golf is about *feel*," he said. "You have to let it flow. Tiger Woods says, 'I just let things happen.'"

"Right," I said. I'd never quite been able to "let it happen." My mind when I was swinging was like a boxful of hamsters running on little wheels to get their food.

He looked at me without high expectations, I thought, and turned on his computer. Two pictures came up on the screen— electroencephalographic images of the brains of a professional and of an amateur in the midst of hitting golf shots. In these images, he explained, green and blue represented the activity of the limbic system, or the parts of the brain that deal with feeling, appetite, and desire. Red recorded activity in the cortex, or the consciously thinking part of the brain.

The picture of the brain of the professional was full of elegant swirls of green and blue and looked like a photograph of the world's oceans taken from space. It had serenity and naturalness.

In the picture of the amateur's brain you could see the swirls of green and blue in the background, but the image was mostly red, with jagged, tortured-looking edges. It was as though a bottle of red ink had been dropped from a height on the picture of the professional's brain. I told Dr. Lagier about George Plimpton's terrifying image of himself as a vast tower full of insane and drunken Japanese seamen, all screaming conflicting orders. "Yes, yes!" he said. "Very good."

All of his work is directed at removing thought and developing feel in the golf swing. "A professional golfer must fulfill three roles," he said. "He must be a Captain of Industry with respect to logistics and business, a Thinker with respect to strategy and the assessment of each shot, and a Worker, who does what is ordered by the Thinker. All require a different cast of mind and none must interfere with the other. What is clear is that the Thinker must know at all times what his objectives are, what are the obstacles to achieving them, and what is the best that he can do in the precise circumstances he is in at the moment. If the tension is high and his breathing is short and his muscles are tight, he will not be able to do what he normally does on the practice range. Maybe he needs a less ambitious shot. The Thinker must make this decision, and when the decision is made, he must depart and allow the Worker to accomplish his appointed task only through *feel.*"

At the time I saw Dr. Lagier he was working with Rafael Jacquelin and a few other French pros, the Argentineans Romero and Cabrera, several Spaniards, including the leading young amateur in Spain, and a number of others who do not wish it to be known that they consult a mind doctor. He is uniquely qualified for his job. He is a neurophysician, a psychoanalyst, and a former athlete who skied competitively. Much of his professional and academic work has been directed toward optimizing performance in sport. He taught in France and then in Texas, but teaching began to demoralize him and he returned to Europe. One day at the Volvo Masters in Andalusia he ran into a former student from France, the wife of Jean Van de Velde. She suggested that he work with her husband, which he did, helping him to advance slowly upward until he played immaculate golf at Carnoustie in the 1999 British Open before imploding in front of the world in the tall grass and water of the seventy-second hole and then losing in a play-off to Paul Lawrie.

Dr. Lagier's work is detailed, analytical, and laborious. If, as the writer Edmund White has observed, the two principal strands of psychotherapy follow two of America's founding Christian religions—quiet, introspective Puritanism, based on a lifetime of devotion and good works, and Evangelism with its shouts and fits and immersion in water and instant salvation—then Dr. Lagier is on the Puritan path. "You can give the player a kind of baptism—there are ways of doing it and it's not so difficult—and he may feel wonderful for a shot, a round, or even a season. But when he comes out of it, as he must, he will need more water, and still more subsequently, the returns ever-diminishing."

When Dr. Lagier begins working with a player, he assesses all the principal aspects of his game—organizational, including the people he has around him, how competent they are, and how well they work together; physical, which is long game, short game, putting, suppleness, and general fitness; and mental, which includes the capacity to handle pressure, dedication, clarity of thought, the setting of objectives, and desire—and then sets realistic objectives in each of these departments. He showed me how he does this by bringing up a computer image representing a Spanish pro he was just then starting to work with, a mandala-like circle divided into triangular sections representing each department of his game, the triangle's points all meeting in the circle's center. Lines crossed the triangles at three points, the innermost one representing the player's current position, the next one representing the point he might realistically reach with dedicated and productive work, and the outermost line representing a notional perfection.

"The path of all this," he says, "is from understanding, to imagining, to feeling. The player must first of all be able to understand what he is doing, including such basic things as how to play all the various shots he will encounter, and what he wants to do. He must then be able to imagine himself doing it. Phil Mickelson, for example, is right-handed, but when he stood facing his father as a boy and watched his swing, he imagined himself doing what his father was doing and produced a mirror image, or left-handed swing. The golf swing is the only action he performs left-handed, and it comes from an act of imagining. Once the player has understood and imagined, he can arrive at feel. Tiger is exceptionally sensitive to this. I was with him for a couple of hours on the practice range at the British Open at Sandwich. You could see him watching the flight of each ball and remembering *precisely* the actions and mental sensations that produced each particular result. He is constantly refining his sense of feel. That day he was using mind and eye and body. If you use video, the image you see is only useful to you if you can see it within about five seconds of hitting the shot, because beyond that time the memory of the feeling that produced it will have faded."

Of the many things that can shatter a player's well-being and capacity to produce good results, an overconcentration on technique is perhaps the most insidiously destructive. Because of this he often finds himself at odds with swing coaches. "If a swing coach proposes introducing a change, I want to know what the objective is, how long it will take the player to integrate it into his game, and if in the end it will truly be worth it. I think sometimes the swing coaches don't think of the consequences of what they do. I have seen them on the practice ranges at tournaments waiting like predators and then coming out when the television cameras are on to manipulate a player's grip or stance or swing plane, sometimes just before they go out on the course. It's obvious that this can be catastrophic. Sometimes the idiosyncrasies of a player's swing can be so deeply established within them that to try to tamper with them can bring about a complete unraveling."

The job, as with any program of psychoanalysis, involves voluminous and detailed observation. He uses video and computer software to compare such things as tempo and swing length on the practice range and in different tournament situations. He times the players over each shot on certain tournament days to measure how consistent they are. He said that the time that Mike Weir stood over his putts on the final day of the 2003 Masters, which he won, varied by no more than four-tenths of a second, except for his approach putt on sixteen, over which he stood for almost two seconds longer. It was, noted one of the commentators, the only poor putt he hit that day. Dr. Lagier assesses players' psychological and physical symptoms under pressure. In one case he discovered that one of his players was so traumatized by tee shots that his pulse shot up to 180 beats per minute solely in reaching to take his driver out of his bag. Sometimes Dr. Lagier will simulate this and other high-pressure tournament situations on the practice range by medically inducing an accelerated heart rate so that the players will be familiar with this feeling and know the kind of shot to hit when they experience it. Sometimes he must administer psychological first aid. One of his players was close to the lead going into the last round of a European tour event and arrived at the course looking tense, pale, and withdrawn. After persistent questioning the player revealed that that morning he'd had a dispute with his girlfriend. He said he was fine and ready to play but clearly wasn't. Dr. Lagier brought the caddy in and told him and the player that the first eight holes of the round were likely to be awful and that they should do their best to get through them in an emergency mode of the most conservative shot-making accompanied by low expectations. If they could hold it together for those eight holes, they might still get a good result. Which they did.

I was never going to get any of this, of course, but Dr. Lagier did invite me down to the practice range to hit a few shots. I hit pitching wedges down to a flag around one hundred yards away. He stood behind me, noting the distance each ball was from the flag and immediately asking "Why?" whenever I hit an ugly one. He saw in each case a shortened backswing or accelerated rhythm or some other manifestation of ill-being or panic and wanted me to register in the immediate aftermath a clear sense of the sensations that had gone into producing these swings and the reasons behind them. A swing, he said, never precisely repeats. The proportions of a signature will remain the same no matter how small or large the writer makes it, but a person will not duplicate once in a thousand times in all neuromuscular detail the action of lifting a glass to his lips. The outer form or style will be the same, but the detail of each movement is different.

We moved to the putting green. Of all the players I know somewhere within my vicinity of ability, I am the worst putter. I once prepared carefully for a three-day tournament with some friends and won it, but averaged forty-two putts per round. In one hysterical display on another occasion I putted nineteen times over six holes. After I'd hit two putts on the practice green in Seville, Dr. Lagier stopped me. "There is one thing immediately clear," he said. "If you are going to continue with this putting stroke, you will have to practice a lot because you are hitting the ball almost entirely with your hands and wrists, and the muscles and nerves between the thumb and forefinger, on which your stroke depends, are among the most tiny and complex in the body and are therefore highly susceptible to variation. This is why the putting strokes of professionals are in most cases led by their shoulders."

"The appalling thing is that I thought I actually *was* putting with my shoulders," I said.

"Well, you're not," he said.

I asked him if he'd mind looking at a few chip shots, at which I excel even more negatively than at putting. He told me to drop a couple of balls, tell me the hole I was aiming for and the distance from it I might reasonably expect to leave the ball.

"I am so bad at this that I have no expectations at all and no means of giving you a figure."

"Try," he said.

"Maybe eighteen feet?"

He laughed. "Okay, then. Eighteen feet. Hit the shot."

I was using a pitching wedge from a slight downhill lie and hit the ball around twenty-five feet past the hole from maybe thirty-five yards.

"Hit it again," he said.

The ball rolled past the hole again, but this time he marked the spot where it landed with a tee.

"Now hit a sand wedge," he said.

I did and watched the ball stop around four feet past the hole. He marked the landing point of this one as well, which was within a foot of where the shot with the pitching wedge had landed. It was embarrassing. After nearly forty years of hitting golf shots I had no idea of the distance balls hit by different clubs rolled on the green. In the progression of understanding, imagining, and feeling, I had not even knocked on the first door. It was a revelation.

8

.

Mr. O'Grady

All through my life I'd played golf on courses I'd traveled to by public transport and where I'd changed shoes on a bench. I began to experience a different, more rarefied form of the game when I began to
write about it. I wrote several travel articles for *Golf World* and was
now flying first or business class to other continents to play on championship courses designed by superstars and groomed, it seemed,
with scissors. I'd stay in $500-per-night rooms in resorts that pro-
moted themselves with laminated brochures decorated with photographs of rolling fairways in dawn light, soft-focus dining rooms,
slender, elegant women in white gowns administering massages, and
with phrases such as "To be a success you need a little pampering
sometimes." I had the idea that I shouldn't be complicitous in this,

but I wanted to see those countries and play those courses I was being invited to and would be unlikely to do so if I had to finance it myself.

I went to Thailand and to Kenya, where I played with my caddy and where the trees were full of monkeys. I went to Palm Springs, an abstract, rather provisional playground in the desert where the golf courses are made of blue lakes and vibrantly green fairways sculpted from a harsh wilderness where rattlesnakes once slithered in the gray dust. Water is so scarce that plants have learned to secrete a substance that kills any other vegetation attempting to grow near them. I played Mission Hills there, jackrabbits with ears the size of unhusked corn standing at the edges of the fairways. I also played the grand, sometimes sadistic PGA West, where Lee Trevino won $175,000 with a hole in one during a skins game on the island-green, par-three seventeenth. I traveled along the north coast of Ireland and played the brutal Portrush, which made me understand a little of how truly grueling must be the four days of the British Open, and Royal County Down, which with its rolls and colors and vistas seemed to have been painted on the land. I played nine holes at Mediterraneo in Castellón with the ebullient Sergio Garcia in the summer before he turned pro, when his handicap was plus six—a world record, he had been told.

In 1995 I played Oak Hill in Rochester, New York, for a piece on that year's Ryder Cup. I was accompanied by the club president, who took me to a spot in the trees on the nearly six-hundred-yard-long thirteenth to describe a shot struck by Severiano Ballesteros during a U.S. Open. He was about forty yards into these woods on

the left, with a ten-yard-wide, perhaps-ten-feet-high corridor leading out between the trees to the fairway. This corridor was at an
angle of around 135 degrees to the hole. Nearly anyone else would
simply have punched the ball back out to the fairway, but Ballesteros
took out a three wood, hit it low off the dirt and leaves through the
gap, and when the ball got out into the open, it rose high into the air
and took the 135-degree left turn to finish around 260 yards up the
hole in the center of the fairway. It was the most astonishing thing,
said the president, that he'd ever seen on a golf course.

In the summer of 2004 I drove across the United States to reac-
quaint myself with it three decades after leaving it and then to write a
book about how it looked to me. Along the way I played some of its
finest courses. I played Oakland Hills in the suburbs of Detroit, site
of that year's Ryder Cup, called The Monster by Ben Hogan after he
won the 1951 U.S. Open there. He called it that after Robert Trent
Jones Sr. had amended the original Donald Ross design with severely
tiered greens and a narrowing of the fairways in the landing area for
drives with bunkers like images out of a Rorschach test in which a
level lie almost never occurs. At times on these vast greens you can
feel you are wandering among windblown drifts in an Alaskan snow-
field. A pin on an upper tier can seem to be on another story. This is
one of America's great and venerable institutions, started with money
from auto tycoons, its clubhouse based on George Washington's
home at Mount Vernon, its first pro Walter Hagen. It's hosted six
U.S. Opens and two PGAs. Gary Player, Jack Nicklaus, and Arnold
Palmer have all won there. It is exacting, varied, honest, and as immaculately presented as a White House dinner.

A few days later I went around the deeply seductive Spyglass Hill in Monterey, named in honor of Robert Louis Stevenson's happy wanderings in this place just south of John Steinbeck's hometown, which is now one of the world's largest gated communities. Spyglass Hill, I was told, was four or five shots harder than its near neighbor Pebble Beach. I went out to the first tee alone, where the starter asked me if I would like to play with two "employees," a man and a woman. The man had already hit. I said I would like that and then decided to display my golfing worldliness by saying that I had just come from playing a course authored, or at least part-authored by Robert Trent Jones Sr., as is Spyglass Hill. "Which one was that?" asked the man, lounging in his buggy. "Oakland Hills," I said. "I know it well," he said. "I played in the U.S. Amateur there." I looked out toward the fairway and saw a tiny white speck, his drive, 320 yards out, perhaps two yards right of center. I was to learn that his name was Buzz Miller, and that he was a libertine-athlete who drove a red sports car and traded in private jets and was in Monterey to play in the Northern California Amateur, thinking, at forty-nine, of turning pro and going on the Champions' Tour. Golf, I thought, is humbling enough without my actively accelerating and augmenting the process by vacuously boasting to my betters.

I played Trent Jones Sr.'s Grand National in Alabama off the back tees, a decision I regretted somewhat when I came to a 225-yard par three with a small green surrounded on 354 of its circumference's 360 degrees by a lake, that day playing straight into the wind. How many golfers in the world could stand on such a tee feeling they had an even chance of evading the water? The Grand National is part of a chain of Trent Jones Sr. high-quality public courses stretching across the state and built with the state's pension fund, a risk that has come to enrich its senior citizenry. I turned off the road to Charleston, South Carolina, to play Pete Dye's Ocean Course at Kiawah Island, site of the 1991 Ryder Cup, as bracing and enlivening as any British or Irish links but complicated by long wastelands of sand along the holes' borders and a waterway system as intricate as an ant colony. I made an attempt at duplicating the five-foot putt on the eighteenth Bernhard Langer faced to retain the Ryder Cup, and missed it as well.

The morning after listening to louche rhythm and blues in the Continental Bar in Austin, Texas, I drove west to Spicewood to Willie Nelson's nine-hole course, the Pedernales Golf Club, which I had first heard about in an interview with Dennis Hopper. I played there on a brutally hot afternoon in July, just before its owner began a tour of minor league baseball parks with Bob Dylan. Afterward I went into the pro shop, festooned with gold records in frames, Nelson family pictures, and signed photographs of various personages, including one of Alan Shepard hitting his six iron on the moon. Next door is Willie Nelson's recording studio, and his tour bus was being hosed down in the parking lot. The course was sequestered by the government when he was having trouble with the tax authorities, but a wealthy benefactor purchased it and restored it to him. On the back of the scorecard are listed various local rules: "When another player is shooting no player should talk, whistle, hum, click coins, or pass gas"; "No more than twelve in your foursome"; "Excessive displays of affection are discouraged." They believe there that a lost ball should not incur a penalty as it is not actually lost but will in fact be found by someone and will then have been stolen. "Who wrote these rules?" I asked the man in the pro shop. He sighed a little. "Willie," he said then.

I went on an extravagantly luxurious trip to Hawaii with a group of journalists that included Lord Bill Deedes, once editor of the London *Daily Telegraph* and previous to that a minister in one of Churchill's governments. I imagined not taking well to a Tory peer and friend of the Thatchers', but he was fine and amusing company, with views that surprised me about Africa, the IMF, and Ireland. I asked him who was the best speaker he'd ever heard. "Lloyd George," he said. He might have said Disraeli or Pitt the Younger or Thomas Jefferson, so much a figure of antiquity did Lloyd George seem to me. We played Mauna Lani, site of several Seniors' skins games, and a great cliffside Nicklaus course on Lanai.

Steve Carr, who'd first told me about Dr. Paul Lagier, was on the trip with me, and I played several rounds with him.

"Have you ever dreamed about golf?" he asked me one afternoon as we were walking along after our tee shots.

"Yes, I have," I said. "Quite often."

"I can tell you what you dreamed."

"Go on."

"You are on the first tee waiting to hit your drive. The course is open and inviting and you can't wait to hit your first shot, but when you get up on the tee, walls and doors start appearing so that you can't take a backswing, or there is a tiny door set at an extreme angle to the fairway which you have to hit the ball through. More and more things appear to thwart you, the ball dropping off the tee, the club breaking apart in your hands. The dream fades away as you keep trying to hit your drive and with new obstacles appearing to stop you."

He was right. This was one of the archetypes of my dream life, like the unprepared-for exam. John Updike has written a short essay about this affliction, in which golf balls can suddenly become cylindrical—"a roll of coins in a paper wrapper, or a plastic bottle of pills"—and the swing is made "in a straitjacket, through masses of cobweb." Yet "the dreamer," he reports, "surrenders not a particle of hope of making the shot." I had a dream just before beginning this book in which I was waiting on the first tee behind a twoball playing a nine-hundred-and-something-hole match, followed by a Moonie, who was accompanied by Serbs in track-and-field costumes doing sprints on the fairway. I was to play a match with an old friend of mine from Chicago whom I badly wanted to beat, but when our turn came and I took out my driver, I found it was missing the central inset piece on the face. I went running into a vast basement with many doors looking for another driver, the dream ending as I ran deeper and deeper into a darkening underground labyrinth, the route back to the golf course growing more obscure but with my need to strike the ball becoming yet more urgent.

Pros dream differently. Ben Hogan had his dream of a round consisting only of nineteen strokes. Arnold Palmer dreamed of shooting a sixty-five in a tournament he was about to play in and then went out and did it. Those of us who constitute the anonymous masses of golf dream as I do, or as the friend of mine who finds the first tee he is standing on in this repeating dream transformed into a white room with a tiny window high up the wall through which he must propel his ball. He desperately wants to make the shot but thinks he can't get a sufficiently high launch angle with his driver, the only club the author of the dream, his own subconscious, has permitted him.

Another friend of mine, an Irishman from Derry with whom I've played as many rounds of golf as I have with anyone, once awoke from a golf dream and immediately recorded it in a letter, which he sent to me the same morning:

We were playing a long par four, you and I, I don't know where. It was very long and very flat. I had crunched my drive miles up the fairway, absolute miles, and had a sand iron out for a gentle lob to the green and a certain birdie. You were playing your second shot first, and whatever way you hit it, whether it was the slipstream as your ball flew directly over mine, or a slight tremor in the earth from your divot, whatever it was, my ball starts to move. I wait for it to stop but it doesn't. It keeps rolling back down the fairway, the flat fairway, the fairway without the slightest hint of a slope, the fairway so flat it must have been laid with a spirit level. How in the name of Christ can a ball roll back down a flat fairway? I walk after it, sand iron in hand, birdie in the head, and still it keeps rolling, faster and faster. I start to run. I am now chasing the ball. My ball. My ball that less than thirty seconds ago was smiling at the green. Suddenly, in defiance of all natural laws, the ball turns sharp right, a ninety-degree turn for Christ's sake, and heads towards a high hedge (where did that come from?—it wasn't there when we were on the tee), in the middle of which is an arch over a stony path. The arch is a wire affair covered in moss and shrubbery, tasteless in a suburban garden but a cruel and unnecessary folly on a par four. It is studded with discarded golf clubs. The ball stops on the red gravel path beneath the arch. I fish the clubs out of the overgrowth to clear the way for my backswing. I'm now miles from my own clubs and all I have is the sand iron but I figure that if I hood the face and beat the living Jesus out of it, I might yet pull off that birdie. It can only be two hundred and twenty odd yards to the flag. I have a lash and move the ball three feet in front of me. I'm so mad at this stage that I throw the sand iron away from me like a javelin and (this is the best bit) it rips through the air straight into the back of a passing fisherman, catches him right between the shoulder blades. Where did he come from? Doesn't matter. Down he goes like a stone and I wake up.

This is the masterpiece of golf dreams known to me, if dreams can be thus described. It deserves, I think, to become a part of golfing lore, like Francis Ouimet's victory over Ray and Vardon in the 1913 U.S. Open or the invention of perimeter-weighted clubs, for in its senses of catastrophe and injustice, terror and unquenchable hope, it is definitive of the game as we the masses play it. But where does such infernal detail come from? What would an analyst say? Why is the dream archetype for golfers the shot that one yearns to make yet which is made impossible by malign forces beyond his control?

The most spectacular of all my golfing trips was to western Canada, where I traveled in a large group from Kananaskis, near Calgary, to Banff, then up past blue-white glaciers and ice fields to Jasper Park, where Doug Wood hooked his chip shot, and finally across the Rockies by train all the way to Vancouver and then north to Château Whistler, where you can ski in the morning and play golf in the afternoon. These are four world-class golf courses that have a thematic coherence not only because of their mountain settings but also because of their architects. The two oldest, Banff and Jasper, were designed by Stanley Thompson. Robert Trent Jones Sr., the designer of Kananaskis, was apprenticed to Thompson and eventually became his business partner. He was also the father of Robert Trent Jones Jr., the designer of Château Whistler.

My favorite was Banff. It is set a mile high in a mountain wilderness with two rivers running through it, built on topsoil that was hauled up by rail and mule. Thompson designed it by entering the woods with a bottle of gin and sitting down at the base of the pines until he could feel the holes forming in his mind. There are jokes, deceptions, surprises, and overwhelming vistas. Fairways are contoured to follow the shapes of the mountain ranges above them, but sometimes the tees are skewed a little to dupe you into taking the wrong line. Bunkers that you think from out in the fairway are tight to the green flare up, you later discover, forty-five yards short.

These and the mountains destabilize your sense of distance so thoroughly that you can be four or five clubs out, as Gene Sarazen once was, unless you go strictly by the yardage. There is a hole there where you climb a quarter of a mile upward to the old professionals' tee and drive over a river that has come crashing down through waterfalls and rapids and that throws up spray below you like fistfuls of diamonds, the ball falling in a long arc hundreds of feet down onto a bending fairway cut through a forest of pine.

When Thompson had designed the course and laid much of it out, he found a narrow, deep bowl in the landscape with a glacial pond at its base, its surface weirdly mottled from the massive rocks on the pond bed. He rearranged his plans and built a new hole there. It is one of the most memorable and mysterious holes I have ever played, a par three with a carry of 160 yards from the side of a mountain down through eerie blue-green light to the green, the still water reflecting the pine trees, the rock face, and the sky.

I was in the first group out that day. It was bright and warm, the day brilliantly clear, the company genial and entertaining, eagles and hawks soaring above, and great bull elks strolling along the fairways with their harems, sharpening their racks of antlers for the bloody wars of the mating season soon to come. They make a sound described as "bugling," a strange mixture of the plaintive and the fierce. If I was assigned to play only Banff for the rest of my life, I believe I would never tire of it.

What makes a great golf course? For most of my golfing life I'd never faced the question because I'd never played on one. But since I began writing about golf, I'd played on courses designed by Pete

Dye, Donald Ross, Alister Mackenzie, Stanley Thompson, Jack Nicklaus, the Fazios, Arnold Palmer, Trent Jones Sr. and Jr., H. L. Colt, and Old Tom Morris. Golf courses have been laid out over lava beds and desert floor, along cliffsides and in orchards, through rain forest, mountains, woodland, and of course through seaside duneland once used for grazing sheep. They can have the feel of amphitheaters, sculpture parks, high dives, and boxing rings. There can be no objective criteria for comparing them. The making of a golf course is like the creation of a work of fiction. It is an imagined order imposed on, and sometimes against, what is offered by nature. This is true even of links, the most natural of courses. You can see it from the air—the green strips and even greener targets slinking through the pale dunes, the round, gray bunkers scattered like coins dropped from a leaking pocket. At the other extreme is desert golf, with its vast lakes and imported topsoil, the falls and rolls of the land made by earthmoving equipment from an architect's drawing. But to try to judge Pinehurst, for example, as better or worse than Troon is, I think, no more fruitful than attempting the same with Faulkner and Evelyn Waugh.

But as with fiction there are golf courses that are lazy, dull, cheap, tricky, and there are courses that are undeniably magnificent. A great golf course will have in some commonly held sense a beautiful setting and will suggest, even if through contrivance, the beauty and power of nature. It will not reek of corporate capitalization, as in courses set down in real estate developments. It must be kept with evident care and attention to detail and be of sufficient length to bring into play the full range of clubs. An architect and the greenkeeper who maintains what has been designed will consider the framing, texture, color, and contour offered by the land so that each hole becomes a kind of painting. Each hole thereby has the feeling of being utterly in its own world. A good golf shot feels more splendid on a great hole. It is as though the hole has lent a portion of its grandeur to the shot.

A golf course involves a journey in which the traveler, at least at the beginning, is open, curious, and willing to be engaged, and it should have as much variety as the setting and the architect's personal sensibility allow while retaining the overall unity of a single authorship. A great golf course will have some holes that are co-nundrums, some epics, and some short, intense lyrics, with perhaps an oasis on each nine. There is often humor on a great golf course—as in Thompson's deceiving flared bunkers at Banff, holes made out of unlikely terrain, a small, sly hazard placed just where a cynical, cowardly, or absentminded shot might land. All along the way, as in an allegory, the architect is asking questions of the golfer. Most are fair and democratic enough to offer the possibility of a range of answers so that players of all levels of ability can remain engaged, but you will always best be able to appreciate a great course from the back tees, for it is the professional with whom the architect is most fundamentally in dialogue.

Finally, in my opinion, a great golf course will not, or at least should not, have artificial waterfalls or decorative fountains spewing up from its water hazards. Water in man-made ponds must be kept moving to prevent the accumulation of algae, but there are ways of doing this subtly, so that the hazard does not look like a feature in the landscaped garden of a corporate headquarters. Such features are, I think, ingratiating and trite. They also distract both from the player's concentration on his shot and his feeling of awe and wonder at the course through which he is moving, should it, that is, be otherwise awesome and wondrous. They are like a Britney Spears lyric inserted into Van Morrison's *Astral Weeks.*

In December 1995 I was sent by *Golf World* to Cádiz in southern Spain to play San Roque and Valderrama and then north to play a few courses round Valencia. San Roque, where each year hopeful pros enter the *corrida* of the European Tour qualifying school, is a pretty and playable course, but it has a fountain in one of its water hazards. The great Valderrama, the number one course in continental Europe and the site of the first Ryder Cup to be played outside the United States or Britain, is tough, fascinating, and kept virtually to what I imagine are Augusta standards, though it is flawed too, I think—the seventeenth and eighteenth, for example, and the little rockery and waterfall on the fourth. But none of these are as bad as its insufferable pretentiousness.

I flew on to Valencia. I had a letter with me from a public relations company in London that informed me that I was to be met at the airport by Maria Ruiz of the Valencian tourist authority, who, the letter said, would be pleased to have dinner with me that night. On the way I looked down at the beige and green mountains and occasionally wondered who Maria Ruiz was. I formed tentative pictures. At the airport I collected my golf clubs and suitcase and walked through the arrivals door. I saw then a lovely looking blonde woman in a gray, short-skirted suit holding with some embarrassment a sign that said "Mr. O'Grady." She drove me in her little car through rice fields to the hotel where I was to stay, and we sat in a conservatory there deciding which courses I would play over the next three days, the sky suddenly turning purple and green, huge, low black clouds churning and rolling, a hurricane-like wind blowing the rain like a prolonged drum tattoo against the glass, and the sea smashing against the breaker walls. I couldn't take my eyes off her.

I played Trent Jones Sr.'s El Bosque, set in hills surrounded by orange groves. I thought I might be playing with the pro, but he referred me instead to a short, bald man with glasses named Gonzalo Ruiz de la Torre, "an excellent player," he said. That seemed, I thought, implausible until he drew his club back on the first tee and launched himself at his ball like a striking rattlesnake and sent it sailing over mine. Later that week we drove north out of Valencia accompanied by Maria through light snowfall toward the Bernhard Langer–designed Panoramica, nearly halfway to Barcelona. "It's skying!" Gonzalo exclaimed. He made four attempts with his frozen fingers to insert a token into the ball machine on the practice range before finally succeeding. He opened with two birdies in these excruciating conditions. By the sixth my grips were hard and wet, my glove soaked, the feeling nearly gone in my fingers, my internal organs seeming to be slowly freezing, and my backswing down to Doug Sanders length because of the coldness in my bones and the fear that the club would fly out of my hands. As we walked uphill on the immensely long ninth, Gonzalo, his ears a bright Christmasy red, spoke animatedly of the fascinating holes we would be encountering on the back nine. Would he play golf on an artillery range? I wondered. I suggested that we thaw ourselves out over lunch, by the end of which there was only time to tour by electric cart the back nine of this impressive, immaculately presented course.

I liked both El Bosque and Panoramica very much, but neither were in the same rarefied world as El Saler, set down by Javier Arana in duneland near the rice fields and the Albufera Lake to the south of the city. This is a beautifully flowing, richly imaginative course full of diversity, intelligence, treachery, and spectacular vistas. Each nine starts among pines and then finishes as a links, the wind, the colors, and the translucence of the air changing as the course opens out. The greens are huge, which adds to the sense of grandeur. The fairways have a generous width, but anywhere off them contains either thick, club-snaring grass or the kind of sandy badland of shrubs and ice plants into which you can disappear and then emerge five shots later. At any point your round can suddenly unravel. I watched Darren Clarke take ten strokes on the par five fifteenth during the last round of the 2001 Spanish Open there.

El Saler is authentic, inspired, beautiful, intriguing, and without mediocrity at any point. Above all it is natural, the holes having been found in the rolls and folds of the sandy land. They generate the feelings of surprise and then of inevitability that T. S. Eliot said constituted great poetry. Desmond Muirhead said of Alister Mackenzie's Augusta National that it "is like a woman with superb bone structure. That was Mackenzie's strength—structure. There have been few architects with sufficient ability to make great holes on the land as it stood rather than always reworking the land to make the holes. Mackenzie was one of them." On the evidence of El Saler, Arana was another. Sometimes, as in art, there is an astonishing confluence of material and mind in which the architect surpasses himself and a masterpiece is produced. When Arana finished building El Saler, it is said that he sat down on the first tee and wept, perhaps at its beauty, perhaps because he believed he would never again do so well. I admire it as much as any course I have ever played, including Spyglass Hill, Royal County Down, and Banff.

Maria met me most days for lunch and for dinner. This, it seemed, was part of her job. On the last night I invited her to eat with me and she accepted. Beforehand we sat in a wonderful bar with beamed ceilings and with the walls hung with dark portraits. She spoke of her father. "In a room full of people I always know where he is. I have to know that he feels all right." Lucky man, I thought, to be loved like that, by her.

I went back to London. I'd been with her so regularly during those few days that it seemed odd to be without her. I was living alone then in a little yellow house in London, having parted with Teresa years before. I found reasons to telephone Maria every now and again, the pretext being a detail in the article I was writing. We exchanged a few letters. I sent her a book I'd written. I tried to find ways of seeing her again that would not seem too overtly like pursuit, but she parried every attempt. Finally, seven months later, she called me to say she was going to the Scottish Open at Carnoustie for work purposes. "Will you be there?" she said. I had never reported on a golf tournament in my life and there was no prospect of me reporting on this one. "Yes," I said.

She drove to Edinburgh and once again was waiting for me at an airport. We went to a few bars and had dinner on a little terrace, watching white-faced mimes darting from portal to portal in some inscrutable act, and then drove to Dundee. We sat in my hotel bar until 5 a.m. waiting for the answer to the single, pervasive, all-defining question that had been hanging in the air ever since her phone call. The light fell early on us in my room and we had a glorious day that had the feeling of revelation out in wild, heathery hillland near Perth. She didn't work much at Carnoustie, but when she did, I walked around the course on my own watching the pros. I followed Montgomerie and Woosnam and some Swedes I'd never heard of. I saw from a distance Eamon Darcy's unmistakable whirligig swing on the eighteenth, where Jean Van de Velde later descended through the concentric spheres of a golfing inferno before self-immolating. The course looked impossible, I thought.

Maria and I met on working trips of hers to Prague and Paris. I joined her at the British Open at Troon, where Arnold Palmer had won his sixth major and where a friend of mine from Derry in the north of Ireland had lost his virginity. He was an apprentice electrician in Troon and the event took place beside a bunker on the internationally renowned par three eighth, known as the Postage Stamp. Maria and I went to New York and to Cuba and soon I was living half the time in Valencia. I began to play at El Saler and eventually became a member. I play there now from time to time with a Basque doctor, Miguel Juantegui, who periodically through his life discovers the secret of golf. It hits him suddenly, like Socrates' fits of abstraction. Once it came upon him while he was ascending alone in an elevator in the hospital in Brussels where he was studying to be an ear, nose, and throat specialist. He was there, hair groomed, tie straight, white coat, stethoscope. Something suddenly and dramatically entered his mind about the hip turn. He bent over and began vigorously swinging an imaginary club, making explosive sound effects of the club hitting the ball and it then sizzling like a firework through the air. What he didn't realize until he looked up was that the elevator door had opened and a crowd of people were silently watching him. He tried whistling and scratching his back as though this was all that he had been doing, but he thinks they weren't convinced.

By the summer of 1998, two and a half years after my brief golfing tour around Cádiz and Valencia, Maria and I were expecting the birth of our daughter, Beatriz. A novel of mine called *I Could Read the Sky* had been published the previous year, and I was myopically moving around the foothills of another, which would come to be called *Light*. The work was slow and sometimes harsh. Two, sometimes three afternoons a week I'd go to El Saler and play golf. It was the only thing other than sleep that could silence the book for a while. I'd have some good stretches on the course, but it was difficult for me to put together an entire round there. I longed to break eighty, which I had not yet done at El Saler, before Beatriz was born, for I knew that regular golf was soon to come to an end, as it had for my father after my birth.

I went out alone one hot July afternoon, with the wind coming from the inland plains, an unusual wind called the *poniente,* which carries a brutal, dry, deoxygenated heat. At its worst the *poniente* can make you feel that your eyes are about to melt. Few people were around El Saler that afternoon and I went up onto the first tee alone. As I looked down the fairway, I thought earnestly about bringing in a score under eighty and hit a drive out to the right that rolled off the fairway and stopped behind a tree. I knocked it out onto the fairway and hit a weak, pushed, ugly eight-iron shot short and right of the green, leaving me with a pitch over a bunker that had to stay under the limbs of an overhanging tree. I skulled it over the green, made a mediocre pitch, and two-putted for a triple bogey seven. That's the round over, I thought, at the first station. I parred the next four, with birdie putts sliding just over the edge on three of them. I came to the sixth, the hardest hole on the course, I think—a 445-yard, treeless, wind-exposed par four that rolls through the sandy land to a long green protected by a deep bunker on the right. You drive into a hill, and if you don't hit it long enough, the second shot is blind. The hole falls away along the left into a vicious rough of sand and shrubs in which you can pass what seems a long, cruel afternoon of hacking and searching and getting blinded by sand, with even worse oblivion to the right. The fairway is generous, but the wind reduces it greatly and the tee shot is nerve-racking. I made a reasonable drive but then hit a low, misstruck three iron short left. I ran the next shot up to about eight feet, then rather absentmindedly hit my par putt, missing it. I was four over after six, which was consistent with my handicap.

The front nine closes with two short, cunningly designed par fours with two-tiered greens and a short par three set down in a bowl in the sand. The eighth is inspired, a 330-yard par four running parallel to the sea and made into a left-turning dogleg by the intrusion into the fairway of a sandy, flower-strewn wasteland that is a continuation of the beach, and with the approach complicated by a high dune right and a severely left-sloping green that runs down from the upper tier. The approach takes great precision, particularly if the pin is cut back right. When I began to play this course, I thought these three holes among the easiest, but I now know how exacting is the demand made both on the tees and for the second shots on the two par fours. While for a professional, with his superior control, knowledge of a course is clearly an advantage, for a middling player it can increase the panic because all the dangers are engraved on the mind. A par on the eighth, in particular, is a considerable relief to me. On this day I hit the seventh in regulation but three-putted from the bottom tier for a bogey, then parred eight and nine. I'd shot a five-over-par forty-one.

I walked over to the tenth tee. I met there a retired professor of anthropology who spoke a rich and ornate Spanish, and I asked him if he'd like to join me. I hit a reasonable drive and we strode off together. I bogeyed the hole with a mediocre chip from the back fringe, but then birdied the next two, a long par five and a par three, with a pair of forty-foot putts. I was now four over after twelve and the round was taking on another complexion. On the thirteenth my birdie putt sat on the lip. Around this time I was addressing the ball incorrectly, with feet and hips square to the target, but with the shoulders open and with the right arm stiff. From here, to hit the ball straight, a range of complex and unlikely adjustments must be made to a body moving at violent and unaccustomed speed. I found out about this flaw a week later when I played with Dionisio Garcia, a former member of the Spanish national team, which at the time also included Jose Maria Olazabal. Its consequence on the fourteenth hole when I was just four over par was a horrific tee shot hit way out to the right, nearly to the adjacent fairway. I was left with a five-wood shot from a slightly tight lie over some low pines and a greenside bunker, and I got the ball to the right side of the green. It was the best shot I'd hit that day. The professor waved his arms from the fairway and enthused about it in an agitated way. The birdie putt ran around the hole and sat on the back edge. I was four over with four to play. I could bogey three of the remaining holes and still break eighty.

The back nine closes with a tree-lined, ever-narrowing par five—where Darren Clarke made his ten—a straight par four with out of bounds on the left, a beautiful 190-yard par three with dunes and bunkers and flowering ice plant all around and played straight toward the sea, and finally the eighteenth, a majestic 440-yard, dog-legging par four that begins on an elevated tee that looks out to the sea and then rolls down to an enormous green, dunes and the beach to the right. The wind was rising. I was getting nervous as I faced these holes and found myself standing for a long time over each shot. I hit two solid woods down the fifteenth and was left with an eight or perhaps nine iron into the wind to a rather narrow green from the center of the fairway. My mind was running around like a swarm of gnats. I took the eight thinking of swinging easily and did what my father told me I should never do—I gave up on the shot, fleeing from it halfway through like a man in a bar fearing rejection by a woman he's admired from a distance. It finished short and right, in a bunker. I hit it out and two-putted for a six. I'd used the first of the three bogeys. I parred the next, with the long birdie putt again running up to the hole, rolling around it slowly, and sitting on the edge. I hit a low, unintentional fade with a three iron to the par three seventeenth, an unappealing but effective enough shot that left me with a long putt down from the upper tier. I got a par with a five-foot second putt.

If I ended the round as I had begun it, with a triple bogey, I would not break eighty. This was certainly possible. The eighteenth has out of bounds on the left, and the dunes on the right are covered with ice plant and various other forms of seaside vegetation that obscure golf balls and from which it is nearly impossible to extricate oneself. I hit my drive left of center with a slight draw, and the ball rolled down into a deep bunker that collects balls nearly from the center of the fairway. I was at the forward edge under a high lip. I thought first of a four iron and then of a seven. Had I used either of these clubs the ball would almost certainly have driven into the lip and rolled back into the sand. Unusually for me I made a sensible decision. I knocked a pitching wedge down the left side, then from light rough hit a six iron into the wind about ten feet to the right of the hole. The putt went in for a par and the professor of anthropology emeritus shook my hand, clapped me on the back, and told me in his courtly manner that he was going to have a bottle of wine with his dinner that night and tell his wife all about the wonderful way I had played the back nine at El Saler. I was five over on the front nine and even on the back for a seventy-seven.

After the round I drove over to the Nueve de Octubre hospital where Maria had an appointment with her obstetrician.

"Do you know what happened today?" I said when I saw her.

"What?" she said. She was tired, hot, and eight and a half months pregnant.

"I shot seventy-seven at El Saler. After a triple bogey on the first. Eight birdie putts missed by less than an inch!"

"What else happened today," she said, "is that I had the last of the ultrasound examinations before the birth of our baby. Do you want to know how it was?"

Bragging about golf is truly repulsive. It is like bragging about sex. No one wants to hear about it and the braggart acquires a malodorous aura that stays long in the memory of the recipient. I have had little to brag about regarding golf, so it has been for the most part an easy matter to avoid this obnoxious practice. Yet despite these strictures and Maria's riposte in the hospital, I could not quite bring myself to stay quiet about my round at El Saler. I came home and telephoned my Irish friend who'd dreamed of assassinating the passing fisherman with his sand wedge. I was a little like the matador who ran directly from bed into the bars in the street outside to tell everyone that he'd just made love with Ava Gardner. It did not seem like bragging, as I knew the round had nothing to do with mastery. As was perhaps the case with the matador, it was the uniqueness of the event that was the point. I knew that I would resume my irregular, pedestrian, and sometimes loathsome style of playing, as indeed I did. "I'm sorry," I said to my friend on the other end of the line. "I know this is tedious and probably even distasteful . . ." He listened with as much indulgence and grace as I could have asked for.

I am now, I suppose, not significantly better or worse at golf than I was when I was eighteen. I could fade the ball more consistently then and was better out of sand because I was hitting hundreds of shots from the bunker beside the green that was in front of the starter's office at Edgewater. But I can sometimes effectively both punch and draw the ball now, as I could almost never deliberately do before. After a golfing lifetime of playing with successively inherited sets of my father's that were at least twenty years old, I finally entered the present technological era by getting a new set of Titleist clubs, custom-fitted at their center at the Brampton Park Golf Club in Cambridge. It took me nearly a year to get accustomed to the new style of driver, which makes the head of my previous driver look like a walnut, but if I am playing with a reasonable rhythm, I am now both straighter and longer off the tee. I've collected a few tips along the way, which I continue to use and value, the best two of which are, first, from Jack Nicklaus, to slow down the backswing almost to the point of the ridiculous when out of rhythm—for, as Bobby Jones said, "No one ever swung a golf club too slow"—and, second, from my father, to hit fast downhill putts, and particularly downhill breaking putts, off the toe of the putter, to deaden the impact. This allows you to make an accelerating yet delicate stroke. From my early teenage years when I was addicted to instructional articles in golf magazines and my head was thereby

full of considerations of weight transfer, wrist break, head position, and hip turn, my body seeming to consist of numerous au-
tonomous sections, each moving in contrary, chaotic patterns like
insects escaping from fire, to a stage when most or at least some of
this drip-fed from my mind into my muscles, to a rather grim late-
adolescent period—extending into my thirties—in which I became
afflicted with a completely unsubstantiated vanity, one of the direst
impediments to any form of expression, golf included, in which I
wanted my swing to be a beautiful display nearly irrelevant to the
actual strike, I have now finally managed to reduce the thinking elements of the swing to two—to not lift the left foot on the backswing,
thereby providing a solid base, and to hit with the right hand, as
Tommy Armour advised. This has had the effect of cleansing the
mind somewhat, and the swing that is controlled by it, in the way
that the removal of adjectives and other decorative flourishes from a
sentence can help to reveal its simplicity and power. I am able to
think a bit more realistically now about shots I might once have
taken on without pause, but I am also more fearful. Fear seems to
accumulate with age—fear of not completing one's work, fear of
losing someone, fear of out of bounds. I have learned little about
planning my route through a hole or making good percentage
judgments. I am a little better around the greens as a result of what
Dr. Lagier told me, and while I still face putts, particularly short
putts, with the kind of dread with which I open post-holiday bank
statements, I have made four changes in my putting which have
given me better direction on the greens—I line up square, where I
used to be open, I keep my head over the ball rather than behind it,

I take the club back and through in a straighter line, and I keep my wrists locked through the stroke. I am still too drawn to the spectacular shot and making a good score instead of taking each shot as it comes in a calm way, and have not found a way to absorb or change the anxiety and frustration and loathing of self that go along with this. I cannot entirely clear the mind, bring in nothingness and repose or sustain a sense of ease and simple pleasure on a golf course, unless, of course, everything is going splendidly. I still play rounds as I did then, with a dozen pars or so and maybe a birdie or two interspersed with double and triple bogeys. This, compounded by the game's very nature, keeps alive the lifelong illusion that if I apply myself, I can somehow bring it all under control. This is the comedy and seductiveness of golf.

At times I've felt a powerful urge to try to do something about it, to try to push on to another level. In the early 1990s I told my father that I was thinking of taking lessons when I returned to London. "No, no," he said. "That's not a good idea. You don't need technique. You've got a caddy's swing." I said something similar to my friend Caryl Phillips. "I want to get on top of this game," I said. "I'm going to put in some time." His reaction was as emphatically negative as my father's, though his reasons were different. "There's only room for one obsession," he said. The golf shot, the sentence. One has certainly fascinated me, but the other has been a thing of identity and desire, and though I suppose I am not much closer to the purity of the sentence than I am to the purity of the golf shot, the pursuit of it has driven and shaped my life. I of course cannot say that about golf. So I do not dispute what my golfing and novel-writing friend said to me about the exclusivity of obsession. I am to remain, then, in a golfing purgatory of the middle ranks, dreaming of a single sub-par round that I could replay again and again in my mind the way that men often summon pictures of the women they have known, but ever watching, as in Loudon Wainwright's song:

> Balls drop in the sand trap.
> Balls drop into ponds.
> Oh, balls drop into ponds . . .

9

.

Symposium

Sometime during my exile from golf in the 1970s, I went into a secondhand bookshop in north London and found a copy of a book called *Golf in the Kingdom* by Michael Murphy. It had on its cover an inaccurately drawn pair of hands poised at the top of a backswing. I had never heard of the book before, though it is now one of the classics of golf literature and is also the primary text of a society with branches in each of the fifty states and a number of countries overseas. I read in the little author's biography inside that Murphy was a founder of the Esalen Institute at Big Sur on the California coast, a center dedicated to the study of esoteric aspects of medicine, psychotherapy, Eastern religion, physics, and, subsequent to the fame of Mr. Murphy's book, golf. I bought it, took it home.

In it are a number of short mystical meditations on various aspects of the game, but the bulk of it is composed of a wonderfully compelling fictional narrative of a round of golf played by a tall, bearded teaching pro named Shivas Irons, a pupil of Irons's named MacIver, and a young American whom Murphy names after himself. The round takes place at a Scottish links course bearing many resemblances to Saint Andrews and called Burningbush. Under the otherworldly yet trenchant tutelage of Shivas Irons, Murphy's game disintegrates to the point where he can barely hit the ball, but it then magically reconstitutes itself before the end. It is the story of a journey down into the darkness and up again into the light, with breakdown and liberation between, and by the end Murphy sees with an acuity previously unknown to him. I have read a few golf books awkwardly infused with mysticism, many of them, I would say, derived from this one, but because of the vividness of Murphy's characters, his narrative skill, his wit, and the evident depth of feeling, honesty, and undeviating tenacity with which he tells his story, the mixture here seemed natural, entertaining, and revelatory. Fiction only rarely generates the feeling that the events it depicts must actually have happened, but that is how this book affected me, so real were its characters and so particular was the relating of what they said and did. I could find no other books written by Murphy, though this was one of the better contemporary novels known to me and was certainly the most astonishing and compelling book about golf I'd ever read and was ever likely to read. I learned many years later that John Updike said to its author, "You are like the fan who comes to the ballpark and is then called down out of the stands to bat and to the astonishment of everyone hits a home run."

Near the end of the story, long after the round at Burningbush is over, whiskey flows at a gathering at the house of a friend. The guests dance wild reels around the floor, and Murphy and Shivas Irons erupt into the dark night, head for the links, and play a treacherous, windblown par three after midnight with a pair of featheries and a shillelagh. Shivas has a hole in one.

This has followed a dinner at which the guests have convened, as in Plato's *Symposium,* to discuss love, specifically their love of golf. Peter, the host, declares that he has a name for each of his numerous golfing personalities—"Old Red," for example, and "Palsy" and "Divot." Driven on by whiskey, he stalks metaphor. Golf is an "X-ray of the soul," he says, and a links one long Rorschach test. Finally, triumphantly, it is like marriage. Both require "steadiness of purpose and imagination, long shots and delicate strokes, steady nerves and a certain wild streak. And ye've got to have it *all* goin' or the whole thing goes kaflooey."

Julian, the town doctor and psychiatrist, believes that players should traverse the eighteen holes dancing the Highland fling to live bagpipe music. "Golf is the yoga of the supermind," says a tiny ecologist named Adam. They discuss hitting balls from mountaintop to mountaintop in Peru and how golf courses are exploded gardens.

"Men lovin' men, that's what golf is," declares Agatha, wife of Peter.

As in the *Symposium,* the definitive statement is the final one. "All art and love depend on fascination," says Shivas Irons. "Life is nothin' but a series of fascinations, an odyssey from world to world. And so with golf. An odyssey it is—from hole to hole, adventure after adventure, comic and tragic. The game requires us to join ourselves to the weather, to know the subtle energies that change each day on the links, and the subtle feelin's of those around us. It rewards us when we bring them all together. In all o' that 'tis a microcosm o' the world, a good stage for the drama of our self-discovery. . . . The grace that comes from such a discipline, the extra feel in the hands, the extra strength and knowin', all those special powers ye've felt from time to time, begin to enter our lives. . . . Devoted discipline and grace will bring ye knowin's and powers everywhere, in all your life, in all your works if they're good works, in all your loves if they're good loves. Ye'll come away from the links with a new hold on life, that is certain if ye play the game with all your heart."

I wondered as I read this, and have wondered since, what I would have said had I been at that dinner. One single chance to make a panegyric about an abiding fascination. It seems a grave responsibility. Speaking, like golf, is a variable activity. The same person can be oafishly incoherent or nearly mute one night, the words seeming to turn to vapor as he reaches for them, and as mellifluous as Oscar Wilde the next. I suppose the whiskey would have helped. And of course it is less difficult to speak of something you love, something that has ignited and continues to ignite something inside you. In such cases it can be more difficult to stop speaking than to speak well.

What is it about golf that ignited something within me? In a certain light the question seems absurd. It is a sport, to some only a hobby, and at that a ridiculous hobby. I once read a description of golf reducing it to an activity that "allows fat, spoiled, middle-aged businessmen to dress up like pimps." But for some reason I have felt toward golf that same quickened feeling of inner identification that I have felt toward certain books, and certain people. What are the elements of golf that do this to me? I don't entirely know. Excitement is not constructed. It happens too rapidly to be analyzed. And it arrives whole, rather than in pieces. We know only that we are engaged, that the prospects of fascination appear to be endless, that we want to go on being engaged and fascinated and that we fear or are hostile toward anything or anyone that might prevent us from doing so.

I suppose I, like other golfers, react as I do to the sport because a round of golf is a journey and all journeys are stories and everyone loves stories. Even if made repeatedly over the same terrain, the journey is never the same and the story is therefore always told as if for the first time. Each time, the player sets out with aspirations for a happy ending but with no idea if he will find it. It is full of engrossment, suspense, unpredictability. Along the way the player will need tact, nerve, preparation, patience, skill, imagination, strength, and delicacy to deal with the challenges and illusions and demons and angels and sirens that he meets, hope and despair in constant interplay, with, perhaps, a rare moment of glory. All of these are in some way aspects of himself. We face ourselves all around a golf course, with every shot. The glory, or the dream of it, draws us back to the start of the journey again and again. The despair is hideous and abasing, a kind of conflagration that in the moment of its happening threatens to devour us. We feel we want to lobotomize ourselves with our five irons. It is also comic, if seen from a slight distance. From this there is something to learn.

The player never ceases in the learning of the game. He tries to learn many things, but above all he is trying to align mind and body, so that in the moment of the shot the mind is all body and the body is all mind and intention is finally one with action. It almost never happens. The mechanisms involved in this alignment are profoundly subtle and elusive and fragile. Failure repeatedly succeeds upon failure. Golf reveals the complexity and difficulty of this task more acutely than anything else I know, yet perhaps because of the difficulty, as in revelation or in art, the feeling in those rare moments when everything comes together is wondrous, explosive. For this the striving goes on, the journey is set out upon again. It is a journey of which the player is the only author. Unlike almost all other sports, golf is neither reactive nor collaborative. The player instigates each action in his own time and, when he has done it, finds himself in a place where only he has put himself. It is existential, a game of solitary accountability in which there is nowhere to hide. This gives it a cleanness, a transparency, not present in most of the other things that we do.

I might have said these and perhaps other things while I drank the whiskey and looked at the other golf-deranged faces around me at the dinner. But if I were allowed time to speak about only one thing, it would have been the exhilaration of flight. This is one of the most, perhaps for me the most, elemental pleasures of golf. It is all so improbable—the tiny ball, the tiny target so far away, the peculiar-looking instrument that launches the ball from a still position through human mechanical strength alone in some mystery of physics, so much farther than any other struck object in sport, the shot cracking in the silent arena of the hole like the report from a rifle, the ball sailing over the terrain, high above the tallest trees and dunes, over mists or rivers or hill-land or the backs of whales, still climbing against a backdrop of sky or mountain or the rising or setting sun, the ball seeming to define the land and architecture beneath it, the player seeming to assume the sensation of its flight, until it begins its descent, the destination uncertain, nervously anticipated, the ball gathering speed as it falls and strikes the land finally just in the heart of the target. Or not, as the case may be. Everybody wants in some way to fly. Golf allows you to do it, through the eye and in the spirit.

When I met Tom Watson, I asked him if he'd ever read *Golf in the Kingdom.*

"I have," he said. "And I admired it."

"Do you remember the scene after the round of golf when they go to a house and have dinner and talk about how much they love golf?"

"I do."

"If you were there," I said, "what would you have said?"

"The history of golf has been filled with so many fine men," he said. "There's a great dignity and sense of decency in the game. When you look at other areas of human activity, certainly the quality of the people who have excelled at golf says much, by comparison, about the quality of the game. In all the other American sports—basketball, baseball, football—players are always trying to find ways around the rules. They are even applauded for it. But in golf if you break the rules, you are seen to be less of a person. Honesty is fundamental to it. It is a game of personal reckoning. You have to accept the rules even if you don't like them, you have to absorb your mistakes, learn to contend with anger and doubt, and play without complaint or special pleading. You cannot persuade yourself that you hit a good shot when you have hit a bad one. These are things which when applied to living make you a better person. I think in this way golf can enhance a person, or even transform him."

I telephoned Arnold Palmer in Latrobe, Pennsylvania.

"Have you ever heard of the book *Golf in the Kingdom*?" I asked him.

"I've read it," he said. "And I liked it very much."

"What do you think you might have said had you been at that dinner in Scotland when they talked about what golf meant to them?"

There was a pause, and a sigh perhaps slightly despairing at the scale of the question.

"Golf has been, and is, my life. I was raised in it and I've never left it. My father was a golfer. He taught me everything I know of the game and of life. I owe everything to it, not only what I have, but what I've learned, the joys I've felt in playing it and all the associations with people I've met along the way. It's an individual game, and I suppose that drew me to it. It bears down on you and illuminates character. There's the expression *in vino veritas,* and certainly golf, like alcohol, can bring out the true person that may otherwise be hidden. It's a never-ending quest to accomplish and prevail. I look forward to getting up every morning not only to hitting balls but also to thinking about the game. It's my life. I can't think of it as anything less than that."

When I was planning my 2003–4 journey around America to look at the country again after my long absence, I knew that I would have to go to San Francisco. It had been the site of so much of the invention and activity that defined the America of my youth, but had also been the destination of the last journey I'd made in America before leaving it for Ireland, a road trip in a 1958 Oldsmobile that took in a Zen temple, a belly dancer, and a young boy named Craig Brake, who sang me country songs in the middle of the night after his mother had given my friends and me shelter during a blizzard in western Nebraska. One of these friends was Robert Gregory. The elderly Oldsmobile was his. He drove it all of the twenty-three hundred miles back to Chicago without ever relinquishing the wheel or stopping to sleep. I would see him when I got to San Francisco, I thought.

Might I also, I wondered, find Michael Murphy, whose astonishing book I'd encountered twenty-five years before and who was now in some way guiding me to the end of my own book about the game? I'd heard that he lived in or somewhere near San Francisco. I'd tried the telephone directory, but the Michael Murphy I'd left a message with hadn't replied. I had more fortune with the Esalen Institute, who gave me the number of his secretary, and after a number of calls and e-mails I met him on a fine June day at a waterfront restaurant in Sausalito, just over the Golden Gate Bridge from the city. We talked through the afternoon about his childhood around Salinas and Big Sur; his encounters with Henry Miller and John Steinbeck; his devotion to the Indian mystic, philosopher, and revolutionary Sri Aurobindo, which had begun when he was a student at Stanford and had continued throughout his life; about his first book, *Golf in the Kingdom,* and other books that followed; and about the game itself. He was lucid, cheerful, and fascinating, and the conversation left me feeling surprisingly alert and happy. After lunch we walked uphill to the small studio apartment where he lives. At the door are photographs of Ben Hogan, Bobby Jones, and Babe Ruth. Inside are wooden floors, shelves of books by or about Hegel, Schopenhauer, and Pythagoras, among many others, and a little terrace that looks out toward the bay, where the sea was shining in the afternoon light. "Upper-level monastic" he called his home. We watched the U.S. Open being broadcast from Shinnecock Hills and talked a little about Tiger Woods. "He set out on a quest with an impossible goal. He's faltering now, but through the desert you have to go on the journey towards any mastery. Does he have another leg to his journey? I think he does. He'll never have 2000 again, I don't think, but he has the resources and the knowledge to prevail. His search is utterly gripping to behold. It's like a Tolkien story. He's drawn me back to the professional game in a way that no one else has for a very long time."

The character whose name he shared in *Golf in the Kingdom* did not give testimony on the night of the dinner. Were he to go back in time to that house in Scotland, I asked him, what would he say about the game to the people assembled there?

"I had long had the intuition that sport can be a vehicle for transcendence. In the West we don't have a language for these experiences. In Sanskrit there is a word, *ananda,* which refers to the delight we feel in existence itself. Western languages don't have words to accommodate this. *Joie de vivre* doesn't quite do it. *Ananda* refers in an abstract way to the ineffable joy from which the world comes. In the Upanishads it says, 'From *ananda* we came, in *ananda* we move, to *ananda* we shall return.' The delight that rules the world. We do not have the rich philosophy and the conceptual systems to deal with this, but we do have, for instance, golf. Golf is a particularly amazing venue for the transcendent, for the mysticism of everyday life. When I wrote *Golf in the Kingdom,* I entered the *ananda* realm. It is not just delight, it is the powers and knowings which in Sanskrit are called the *siddhis,* the powers that emerge in yoga. In the Catholic Church they are called charisms. We continually deny ourselves these experiences because of the repressions of our culture and of our religions, or, if they happen in the context of sport, because of our idea of the tough and supercontrolled sportsman. But they emerge in small and large ways in golf, as they do elsewhere in our lives. Golf is a mystery school for Republicans. In the thirty years since I wrote *Golf in the Kingdom,* people have been contacting me and telling me in their shy or halting or sometimes ecstatic ways of their experiences of transcendence on golf courses. A woman wrote of the sun setting and of the sudden appearance of a powerful luminescence over a golf course. A lawyer found he could see with such clarity that a dime on the green four hundred yards away from the tee where he stood was perfectly visible to him. They begin to talk more freely, they have the urge to connect with another about these uncommon, glorious experiences of which I am taking their confession. In this way *Golf in the Kingdom* doesn't yet have an ending. It seems truer to me now than when I wrote it."

Sometimes after a round of golf or in bars late at night, I'd ask friends of mine the question I'd put to Watson, Palmer, and Michael Murphy. Nothing remains in my mind of their answers. Perhaps it is my poor memory or the lateness of the hour or that they hadn't anything ready. It is also true that most people don't have an analytical consciousness traveling along ghostlike in parallel with everything they do. I'd sometimes wondered how my father would have fashioned a statement, though I'd forgotten to ask him whenever I went to visit him. Why do you love it so much? What in you does it express? These were the questions that had remained unasked.

I had three chances to ask them in 1993, the last of them in October when I stopped in Chicago on my way back to London from playing golf in western Canada. It had by then been more than three years since my mother died. My father had begun his long, slow decline long before that, but subsequently, on each of the anniversaries of her death, he had suffered increasingly debilitating crises that had hospitalized him and left him still more frail than before. Throughout these years I was in London hearing news about his health from himself or his doctors or his friends and had to gamble on when was the best time to travel to see him. I had to hope that I would not be too late.

In that year I had visited him in May and then again in August. He'd survived up to then living alone with a woman coming in a few afternoons a week to cook for him. That summer he told me he could no longer go on like that. He hadn't the strength. He was too nervous. I found someone willing to live with him full-time, an intelligent and dignified Filipino woman who in her youth had wanted to become a nurse but had been prevented by her parents from doing so. She seemed to know when to leave him alone and when to give him company. Sometimes in the evenings she brought a small electric piano into his room and sang for him.

I found him in bed in his pajamas when I arrived from Canada, utterly skeletal, his diminished head like a small piece of fruit on the pillow. He no longer dressed for the day and rarely got out of bed. Eating had become a misery. I came and went from his room through the week, talking with him and sometimes playing music for him on a little tape machine. Once I came in to find him standing up with his pajamas around his ankles and a visiting nurse crouched at his feet bathing him. He looked at me as if to say, What do you think of this? He told stories and listened intently and laughed as before, but it was all paler now, and fading. I told him about visiting Tom Watson at Sandwich that summer and about Watson's team winning the Ryder Cup at the Belfry just the week before. I also told him about my extraordinary time in Canada and about the great courses I'd played there, particularly Banff, which I described in operatic language. Perhaps I was excessive. He listened, his eyes widening as I spoke, and then said with some alarm, "You speak as though this was the most amazing experience of your life." He was right. I hadn't the measure of the experience, or of his capacity to hear about it or of how to look at him in the condition he was in.

On the day that I left, I looked into his eyes and saw that they were already half in another world. He'd given up the struggle and didn't seem to mind. The eyes were dreamy and serene. He'd lived straight, so far as I knew. He was square with everyone of importance to him. He had no strength left and there was no point looking for more, for it wouldn't come. Letty, the Filipino woman, was allowing him to die by removing the need to struggle. What could I do to hold him a little longer in the world? My suitcase was at the door, a friend was waiting to drive me to the airport. I told him I had things to do in London, but I also had a book to finish and I could do that in Chicago as well, I supposed, as anywhere else. I would come back the following month and stay with him there while I did the work. "That's fine," he said. I took him up in my arms. His insubstantiality shocked me. He was like a cloud. What had I to offer him now? Already he was drifting away. "Are you afraid of anything?" I asked him. "No," he said. His eyes were wide and looking out beyond me somewhere.

I went back to London. Letty called me a week later to tell me that my father had been engulfed in an entirely sleepless forty-eight-hour-long hallucination during which he barely stopped moving. She barricaded one of the exits from his room with a heap of furniture, but he dismantled it. When I had been there he barely had the strength to stand. He lay down for a little while, but then in the middle of the night she found him roaming again.

"What are you looking for?" she asked him.

"For my checkbook," he said.

"What for?"

"There's a man waiting in the living room and I have to pay him."

"What do you have to pay him for?"

"For my funeral services," he said.

When it was over, he slept for fifteen hours, and when he woke, he was himself again, weak but no longer hallucinating. I called him.

"What was that about?" I asked him.

"I don't know," he said. "But it's left me very tired."

The book I was writing was a novel containing pictures by the photographer Steve Pyke. Three days after that conversation with my father, Steve and I traveled to Ireland together to get the last of the pictures for the book. It was October 15. I was, at this point, living on my own, and when we flew to Dublin, no one knew where we were going. We didn't entirely know ourselves. After we landed we went around the bars. We met a couple of friends in Wynne's Hotel and then walked over to the Flowing Tide, across the street from the Abbey Theater. Just after closing time a cousin of Teresa's whom I hadn't seen in the years since Teresa and I had separated walked through the dim light to our table. I was pleased to see her but she looked preoccupied. She told me that her husband had a message for me. What I didn't know was while I was landing in Dublin, Letty was making calls to a list of numbers I had given her, to my cousins in Chicago, to my home in London, and to several other numbers, including Teresa's, and that Teresa had phoned everyone she knew in Dublin to ask if they'd seen me. Her cousin had been found at the Abbey Theater and, out of all the bars in Dublin, had walked into the one I was in. I went with her to a phone and called her husband. From him I learned my father had died. He'd stood up beside his bed at noon and then sat down again. He told Letty that he couldn't make it. He lay down on the bed then and the life went out of him.

I went back to Chicago and moved around the rooms filled with the furniture of my childhood. It had the feeling of the stillborn about it. Everything was dusted and put away and the bed on which he'd died was neatly made. Bottles of his medicine were on a little tray in the kitchen. I tried to pick up some sense of him in the air but I couldn't. It was vacant. He'd stood on his feet for fifty-five years

looking into people's mouths. He'd won a Charleston contest. He'd
drunk in speakeasies and on the streets of Havana, and when he was
small, he felled a local bully with a lucky punch. He had a gift for
telling stories. He'd shot subpar golf. He'd found a woman who
never ceased to fascinate him. He was kind and steady and severe
and glamorous. He was the one truly heroic figure of my life. He'd
arrived at the point where everything was fading and dimming and
where his mind was tethered to his decrepitude. Now he was free.

At the funeral I looked at the coppery sheen on his coffin and realized that all the things that kept occurring to me to tell him would
forever remain unspoken. I had the idea of getting in his car and living for a while in motels by the side of the road as I headed south,
maybe all the way down through Mexico to Guatemala. I could
write the rest of my book that way maybe. But I didn't do it. I
stayed in Chicago and cleared away his things—his furniture and
pictures and books, his trousers and shoes and hats. I found a
leather box with a loose hinge containing pens and nail files and
combs, fine strands of his silver hair still caught between the teeth.
There was a letter to his father he'd written from the Pacific when
he was with the navy during the war. There was a photograph of
my mother laughing as she faced a wild bear in a forest in North
Carolina. There were key rings, holy medals, and golf scorecards,
one that included a hole-in-one in a round of seventy-six he'd had
when he was sixty-eight. There was a little printed homily about
golf written by someone named David R. Forgan with "From E. J.
O'Grady" typed at the bottom, and there was the note Arnold

Palmer had written to him when I'd played with him at Bay Hill—"To Ed, Sorry you couldn't be here for the golf. Tim was good. Best wishes, Arnold Palmer." There was a poem about fathers and sons that he'd cut from a newspaper, the paper yellow and the edges jagged where his hands had been unsteady, and which I could not read to the end the first or the second or even the fifth time I attempted it.

I'd never asked him what he would have said had he been at the Scottish dinner in Michael Murphy's book. Perhaps if I had, I wouldn't have got an answer, but I think it likelier that he would have tried. Whatever golf is—an escape from quotidian life, a lark, a livelihood, a lifelong dialogue—to speak about it is only a game and I am sure he would have participated because he enjoyed games and they made him laugh. What would he have said? I cannot know. I have only that small printed page with his name typed at the bottom that I found in his leather box. As I sifted through his things, I found several more of them in desk drawers, envelopes, and stuck among the pages of books. Where had they all come from? It read:

GOLF—AN APPRECIATION

It is a science—the study of a lifetime, in which you may exhaust yourself but never your subject. It is a contest, a duel or melee, calling for courage, skill, strategy and self-control. It is a test of temper, a trial of honor, a revealer of character. It affords the chance to play the man and act the gentleman. It means going into God's out-of-doors, getting close to nature, fresh air, exercise, a sweeping away of mental cobwebs, general recreation of the tired tissues. It is a cure for care—an antidote to worry. It includes companionship with friends, social intercourse, opportunity for courtesy, kindliness and generosity to an opponent. It promotes not only physical health but moral force.

This was him on the golf course, I thought, or at least a part of him—though he would have expressed it more simply and directly. He learned and he taught, he searched for ideas, he was genial and entertaining in company, he sought the catharsis of the hard-hit shot in the open air. He was fair, honest, gracious. I knew about his moral force because he'd wasted me with it when I'd lied or been deficient in respect toward my mother. He was drawn both to the solitary trial of self and the chance to compete and win. I think he liked the idea of facing up to the exposure all this entailed. If golf reveals character, as the piece says, then I would say he was vindicated through his relationship to it.

He was better than me in all of this and in the level of his play. If golf reveals character, I find mine stained here and there with petulance, victimhood, envy, and schadenfreude. Also vanity, through the pursuit of the glorious shot instead of the kind of play that wins matches. I can still learn from him in these things. I think of the way he was with a golf club, how balanced and sure and intimate, how taut with concentration, the head down, the hands moving forward and out. I think of him going at it one-handed when he cracked a rib, of the three wood he rifled at the man who had bombarded my mother and me, of that last low line drive he hit to the edge of the green when he was eighty-six. I look for him, for the soundness of his ball-striking, his dignity while enduring bad play, his tenacity and focus, and in the controlled and sure act of faith and release that was his golf swing.